MASTERS OF
DECEPTION

MASTERS OF DECEPTION

The Worldwide White-Collar
Crime Crisis and Ways to Protect Yourself

Louis R. Mizell, Jr.

John Wiley & Sons, Inc.

New York • Chichester • Brisbane • Toronto • Singapore • Weinheim

Library of Congress Cataloging-in-Publication Data:
    Masters of deception : the worldwide white-collar crime crisis
and ways to protect yourself / Louis R. Mizell, Jr.
      p. cm.
    Includes index.
    ISBN 0–471–13355–8 (cloth : alk. paper)
    1. White-collar crimes—United States.   2. White-collar crimes.
I. Title.
HV6769.M59   1996
364.1′68—dc20

FOR THE VICTIMS

About the Author

LOUIS R. MIZELL JR. is an expert on criminal and terrorist tactics, targets, and trends and has been featured on dozens of television and radio shows.

As a former special agent and intelligence officer with the U.S. Department of State, Mizell served in 87 countries including such hot spots as Lebanon, Iran, Chile, Colombia, Peru, and the Philippines. In addition to his investigative and intelligence roles, he was assigned to Secretary of State Cyrus Vance's personal protection team, protected Senator Nancy Kassebaum in El Salvador, and worked at both the 1984 and the 1988 Olympics.

Mizell also served in Vietnam with the U.S. Marine Corps, has a master's degree in law enforcement from the American University, Washington, D.C., and is the author of several books on security and crime.

He has received over 1000 invitations to speak on the topics of terrorism and crime throughout the world and has taught a course on terrorism at American University. He is currently president of Mizell and Company, International Security, a group in Bethesda, Maryland, that collects criminal and terrorist data on 4000 topics.

Contents

CONTENTS

Acknowledgments

To communicate the pervasiveness and the dangers of the white-collar crime epidemic, a lot of good, dedicated people wrestled with mountains of data and toiled night and day for many months. These people—my partners in crime—culled through 40 newspapers a day, contacted police in all 50 dates, checked court records, played phone tag with over 300 sources, and sorted through nearly 350,000 incidents of white-collar crime. To this team of spunky and scrappy professionals, the best of the best, I would like to say thank you; you were a pleasure to work with and won my deepest admiration. Now get some sleep.

Masters of Deception would not have been possible without the enthusiastic endorsement of publisher John Wiley & Sons, Inc. Professional, hard charging, and fun to work with, Jacqueline Urinyi and Myles Thompson said "Do it!" and made this book happen. Their upbeat, positive attitude was contagious and much appreciated.

Professional and attentive to detail, Cape Cod Compositors

proved they were masters of their craft. A special thank you to Missy Garnett, Susan Sinnott, Judy Donathan, Joanne Jesse, and Mike Rogers.

John Willig, my literary agent, is kind enough to laugh at my agent jokes and always takes my interests to heart. I appreciate this very much.

Becky Boyd, my dedicated administrative assistant and loyal friend, makes us all toe the line and has the uncanny ability to anticipate our every need. Diplomatically keeping the dreaded bureaucracy off my back, Becky emits enough energy to light up New York and is the best at everything she does. You are wonderful and much appreciated.

The personification of honesty and good character, my good friend Patrick Friel, lean and mean, is living proof that there is a lot of good in this world. After writing this book I needed the assurance.

Mrs. Noreen Beavers—you are an amazing woman. When there's a tight deadline on a critical job, give it to a scrappy senior par excellence.

To Erica Walters, the youngest member of my staff, you've got a great future. Keep writing, stay disciplined.

To Peter Roche, my partner in crime in 20 countries—ain't life a wonderful adventure!

A package of dynamite, Lisa Landi, Notre Dame graduate and expert on serial murderers, has a bright future in law enforcement. I admire your spirit.

A financial consultant and banking expert, my friend James Kent Hamilton contributed much to this book. Your professionalism was much appreciated.

Jack M. Burkman, banking counsel to Congressman

Rick Lazio, and John J. Byrne, of the American Bankers Association, were very helpful.

Maggie Watt—thank you for all the help on the medical chapter and for taking care of the animals.

Guardian angels in a time of need, Robin and Michael Pomeroy provided a much needed sanctuary. Thank you.

To Patty Raine—thank you for your friendship and advice.

To my parents—don't worry, I'll get a real job someday. Maybe.

As with most books, *Masters of Deception* had a lot of unsung heroes who contributed invaluable time, spirit, and professionalism. I genuinely believe that their efforts will help put a stop to white-collar crime. Thank you, thank you, thank you: Carol Stricker, Tim Dixon, Jim Grady, Jeff Bozworth, Tony Deibler, Victoria Time, Bob Stockman, Robin Barbour, Vicki Brown, Jan Mosca, Rebecca Frailey, "Boss" White, John McKennan, Aura Lippincott, Rick Watts, William Zinmeister, Bill Elderbaum, William Penn, Grace Goodier, Dave Haas, Isabelle Claxton, Dane Barnhard, Barry Covington, Bob Ross, Rick Young, Bill Ottley, Sheri Bochantin, Chris and Allegra Leibengood, Tara Clifford, Lisa Fentress, Mike and Peggy Wile, Greg and Hsiao Hsien, R.L.M., Steve Mayes, Bleu Lawless, Stacey Patterson, Nick Dale, Bill Trites, Miller Young, Esther Mizell, Suzanne Conway, Mike McDonald, Betty Baker, Penny Reid, Susan Stalick, Karie Newmyer, Laude Cuttier, Shadia Barakat, Jack Gottschalk, Mike Harrington, Gary Saylor, Joe Mallet, Paul Sorenson, Jim McWhirter, Mary Griggs, John Gibbons, Jim Hush, Ray Baysden, Bowman Miller, Sara Schoo, Dennis Bochantin, Jose Hernandez, Dave Gaier, Joe Hemsley, Maureen Becker, John Bedrosian, Jim Frazee, Jimmy Johnson, Hutton Glascoe, Dale Shomper,

ACKNOWLEDGMENTS

John Secan, Liz LaRosa, Thomas Tragert, Julie Bondroff, Jamie Smith, Gretchen Sanders, Sara White, Elizabeth White, Jane Garzilli, Karen Tamzarian, and Reed, Leanna, and "Sissors" Smith.

I would like to say thank you to Jesse, a beautiful golden retriever (you are a good ole dawg), to "Michelle," my gorgeous computer (our intimacy frightens me), and to Dr. Michael Morris, Dr. Benjamin Aaron, Dr. Tim Burke, and the wonderful nurses at the George Washington University Medical Center.

Keep smiling, stay positive, and dare to be honest.

Introduction

Last year hundreds of private investors and nonprofit institutions poured millions of dollars into the purportedly charitable Foundation for New Era Philanthropy, which promised double-your-money returns and altruistic donations. It was a beautiful idea on paper, but the Foundation turned out to be a fraud—a massive pyramid scheme—and hundreds of millions of dollars was lost or misappropriated into greedy pockets. And it wasn't just the hapless who were duped. Many of the investors were seasoned businesspeople and sophisticated institutions.

That scandal was startling but not particularly unique, or even unusual. Right now from large, well-lit offices, white-collar criminals continue to pick our pockets to the tune of $300 billion every year. Hiding behind what is equivalent to a curtain of respectability, these "socially acceptable" criminals rob more from companies and individuals with a pen or keystroke than a street thug can plunder with a high-powered pistol. As masters of deception, today's briefcase bandits wear a smile for a mask and camouflage their criminality with a corporate office.

White-collar crime takes a variety of shapes. Credit card fraud costs U.S. taxpayers nearly $3 billion a year, while fraudulent telemarketers pocket $40 billion. Targeting every conceivable account, armies of crisp-suited financial felons steal billions from pensions, unions, wills, trust funds, museums, libraries, churches, and charities.

Inventing new strains of fraud every day, these people are poised as lawyers, doctors, nurses, insurance salesmen, accountants, fund-raisers, bankers, and sometimes even neighborhood priests, ministers, and rabbis. It's an alarming epidemic that has reached every big city and small town in the United States. We all know someone personally who has been taken to the cleaners. Sometimes it's the elderly or disadvantaged, and just as often it's a company or institution.

Although the white-collar criminal is less notorious than a terrorist, the combustible mixture of greed, arrogance, and ambition can be even more deadly. The fact is that crime in the suites causes more death than crime in the streets.

Thousands of people are put in peril each year because transportation and construction executives reason that it is more profitable to use substandard parts and to ignore safety regulations. Thousands more are injured or killed in white-collar arson-for-insurance and murder-for-insurance plots. And thousands on top of that are endangered or killed because dishonest health-care professionals perform unnecessary operations, knowingly sell, use, or conceal medical equipment with deadly flaws, or practice medicine without a license.

The accounts are startling, but collaring the white-collar

crook is not easy. The likelihood of the suited set being charged, or if charged tried, or if tried, convicted, is relatively small, and the exception to this rule is often treated like a wayward child and merely slapped on the wrist. Corporate criminals don authority like a cloak of armor, they are adept at portraying themselves as victims, and they arrogantly believe that they are above the law.

Attending the best schools, they often get high marks for intellect and low marks for character. In recent years more than 1600 Ivy League graduates—including over one hundred men and women from Harvard University—have been charged with the most heinous of upperworld offenses.

Whether you're the head of a business or an individual with a family to worry about, you need to know what to do to protect yourself—and what not to do. There are standard safeguards that we should all be practicing, and checks and balances that need to be in place. Plus, it helps to be aware of the actual ways that people, companies, and entire industries are victimized every day. There are considerable means by which we can fight back. No one has to shrug and remain passive.

Masters of Deception takes you through scores of actual cases of white-collar crime in sectors like health care, charity work, business, and religion, and explains what the trends mean, who the bad guys are, and whom you can trust. And in case you aren't convinced of the problem after reading the startling accounts in these chapters, there are enough chronicled incidents in the Appendix to make your skin crawl.

But before you fire your doctor, lawyer, accountant, and minister out of fear, and before you hide your money in the backyard under the tree, remember that if you are informed—if you know the statistics and what to watch out for—you will be less likely to be victimized. After reading this book, the bells and whistles should go off in your head anytime you're a potential dupe.

I've dedicated this book to the victims of white-collar crime because they have the scars to back me up, but I've *written* this book for everyone else, so that they can empower themselves with enough knowledge to never be a victim.

CHAPTER 1

Stealing Education

It's the same story everywhere.

We'd like to hire more teachers and provide better security for our schools, but there isn't enough money.

These courses and services are important, but the school can't afford them.

There's no money in the budget for new books and computers.

Ever wonder why the most powerful country in the world never has enough money for education? A big part of the answer is very simple. Dishonest school administrators, educators, and others are stealing or wasting more than $8 *billion* each year. This is an $8 billion loss that does not need to occur.

The Big Picture

Every year an average of $160 million is embezzled and stolen from schools and colleges in each of our 50 states. $160,000,000! How many new programs, raises, and scholarships could each state provide with an extra $160 million? How much could the educational system in the United States be improved with an extra $8 billion?

Tens of thousands of criminals are stealing from the educational coffers. And even a quick glance at the data illustrates that one hundred crooks can use one hundred different tactics to steal from one hundred different educational accounts.

Nearly $4 billion is siphoned annually from a wide variety of financial aid programs. More than $2.5 billion is lost each year because of deadbeat students defaulting on school loans. And hundreds of millions of dollars are embezzled from educational accounts each year by dishonest employees.

Many of the $100,000 to $4 million embezzlements have caused massive layoffs and even school closings. The Robert White School in Boston, Massachusetts, a last-ditch alternative school for troubled inner-city children, was forced to close in 1993 when the director, Melvin Lawrence, embezzled $105,000. Lawrence, a doctoral candidate in the Boston University School of Education, overbilled the city by inflating the attendance figures and by writing $105,000 in school checks to himself. On January 20, 1995, in Wayne County, Michigan, Mary Ann Brueggemann, a 59-year-old treasurer for the Holy Cross Lutheran Elementary School, pleaded no contest to embezzling $363,000. The embezzlement forced the 67-year-old school to close.

Like most white-collar offenses, Brueggemann's crimes could have been prevented with tighter internal controls. Brueggemann was able to write 185 highly suspicious checks—including many that were written to herself or to "cash"—because the school required only Brueggemann's signature on the checks. If two signatures had been required for each check, the $363,000 embezzlement would have been much more difficult to pull off.

In the past decade, hundreds of dishonest employees and administrators have pocketed the donations that private citizens contributed to their alma maters. In 1993 the Baptist-affiliated Mississippi College accused Lewis Nobles, 67, its former president, with pocketing about $3 million in contributions. The lawsuit claimed that Nobles personally solicited contributions, issued bogus receipts, and then deposited the money in his own bank accounts. Nobles, who once fired a football coach because his pending divorce might reflect badly on the college, allegedly spent the donations on personal investments, gifts, and prostitutes.

Multi-million dollar research grants have also been lucrative targets for the unscrupulous. At the University of California, Los Angeles, a professor embezzled $450,000 of UCLA's research grant money. Prosecutors proved that Professor Cavour W. Yeh, 55, had hired unqualified relatives to work on government grants, turned in bogus employment applications for them, and received kickbacks from their salaries. UCLA and the federal government paid Yeh and his relatives $450,000 of the taxpayers' money for work that was never performed.

Tens of thousands of white-collar crimes committed in the educational environment prove that no budget is immune to theft and no account is secured. White-collar crooks have embezzled millions of dollars from even disabled children, AIDS and cancer research, and the poor.

In Virginia, a 25-year-old cashier for the Richmond State School was charged with stealing $68,000 in wages earned by mentally and physically impaired students. The missing money had been earned by the special students who have jobs filling one-pound boxes with nails, assembling plastic cup lids, and working in the school laundry. In Kent, Washington, the director of a school for children with dyslexia and attention deficit disorders siphoned off $343,627 of the school's money and used the funds for personal investments. And in Washington, D.C., an administrator with the public school system embezzled $54,000 from the Neediest Kids charity and used the money to buy fur coats, jewelry, and other luxuries from the Home Shopping Network.

Computer Fraud and Fake Work Scams

As schools increasingly use computers to balance their budgets, pay bills, and transfer money, the number of computer-related thefts is also increasing.

At the Florida Institute of Technology, a fourth-year humanities student employed by the school's Housing and Student Activities Department set up a two-year computer scam that allegedly netted him $31,019. By changing computer records, the student was able to falsely credit his account and the account of other students with institute money.

Scores of administrators have stolen millions of dollars from high schools and colleges using versions of the phantom employee and fake work scams.

In one case, a local school system paid $127,000 to have asbestos removed from a high school because an administrator claimed that inspectors had ordered the removal for health reasons. There were four problems with this contract:

1. There was no asbestos in the school;
2. No health official ever inspected the school;
3. Asbestos-removal contractors never worked in the school; and
4. The administrator deposited $127,000 into his own account.

On February 22, 1995, two former administrators with UCLA's radiology department were indicted for allegedly embezzling more than $600,000 by duping the university into paying two employment agencies, secretly established by the administrators, for work that was never performed. Approximately $220,000 of the stolen funds was used to pay construction workers who built a 2000-square-foot addition on one administrator's home.

Many school administrators have been accused of running several scams at once. On March 31, 1995, prosecutors in New York City charged that Stuart Possner, principal of Public School 100, stole $76,000 from the school system using a wide variety of illegal schemes. The lengthy indictment alleged that Possner, the 1992 Principal of the Year in his district, pocketed $11,000 that his students had raised through the sale of candy, stole cash proceeds from the school's Valentine's Day dance, and plundered school supplies worth $4000 for use at the summer camp he operated in the Poconos. The indictment also charged that he got paid for pretending to work as a supervisor of an after-school program when he was actually working as a principal for a Jewish religious school and that he forced school employees to make party favors, during working hours, for his son's bar mitzvah and his daughter's sweet 16 party.

Wielding prestige as their weapon, white-collar criminals are pocketing billions of dollars earmarked for schools and colleges and are pilfering our most valuable national treasure—education.

The Embezzlers

Prince George's County, Maryland

On March 3, 1994, Eugene N. Carbaugh pleaded guilty to embezzling an astonishing $1,054,000 while working as chief of the accounts payable department for the Prince George's County, Maryland, school system. Circuit Judge James P. Salmon told the balding, 63-year-old man that he had done "a great deal of harm to the schoolchildren" and ordered him to spend the next five years in prison.

A trusted school system employee of 24 years, Carbaugh lived with his wife in a comfortable two-story home near the Chesapeake Bay, raised two daughters, and typically wore inexpensive polyester suits. "He was a nice, low-profile kind of guy who didn't seem rich," said an acquaintance. "He played nickel-ante poker and bought a few lottery tickets, but I don't think he had a drug or a gambling problem."

Like most white-collar criminals, Carbaugh had successfully embezzled money for many years before being caught, and like most white-collar criminals, he was caught more by accident than by design.

During his 12 years as an accounts payable chief, Carbaugh used his position to have 74 checks—some as high as $18,000—issued to fake companies he controlled. After opening a bank account for a phony fuel oil company called BPC/PEPCO, Carbaugh had his unwitting employees write checks to pay bogus invoices. Since the school system pays millions of dollars for utilities and heating oil, the employees had no reason to be suspicious. The checks would be sent to Carbaugh's post office box and he would then deposit the checks in the BPC/PEPCO account.

Stealing the funds from the pockets of schoolchildren, Carbaugh then laundered the money through several legitimate businesses he owned, including a video rental shop and a chain of dry-cleaning stores. Employees of these businesses would later tell police that Carbaugh always purchased equipment with cash.

In 1992 Carbaugh's wife accused him of adultery and filed for divorce. After he and his wife separated, he moved from his comfortable home near the bay to a mobile home park within sight and scent of the city dump. Medicating his stress with stolen money, he soon went on a check-writing binge. He had four checks totaling $24,900 written from the school system to his companies within three weeks of moving into his new quarters. Like a drug addict, Carbaugh was beginning to require larger and more frequent dosages. The more money he stole, the more he wanted.

Carbaugh was finally discovered in 1993 when he tried to deposit yet another school system check into his personal business account. Only this time, a conscientious bank teller called the school system to verify the check. The clerk was informed that Carbaugh and the company listed on the check were not authorized vendors. One smart bank teller had made one phone call, and a crook's world came crumbling down with a crash.

Unfortunately, Eugene N. Carbaugh is only one of *thousands* of people who have embezzled huge amounts of money from the educational environment. During the past decade dozens of men and women have stolen $1 million or more from schools and colleges in the United States. Hundreds of corrupt individuals have embezzled sums of $100,000 or more, and thousands of dishonest men and women have quietly siphoned sums ranging from $1000 to $100,000.

Incredibly, several individuals have managed to embezzle amounts totaling $2 million, $3 million, $4 million, and more! The guilty parties in these cases are almost always respected, well-liked individuals who are in positions of trust and have easy access to the money. When and if an embezzler is caught, shocked coworkers inevitably comment that "She didn't seem like the type" or "He was the nicest man."

Newport-Mesa Unified School District, California

In Santa Ana, California, on June 25, 1993, Stephen A. Wagner, a baby-faced 41-year-old former chief financial officer for the Newport-Mesa Unified School District, was convicted of embezzling $3.5 million in school funds. As a result of the embezzlement the school district was forced to lay off 209 employees (including 59 teachers) and reduce the number of classroom aides by 50 percent.

Diverting school funds to support a lavish lifestyle, Wagner purchased a million-dollar mansion in Newport Beach, a Rolls-Royce, two Mercedes-Benzes—one with a license plate that read "just-cuz"—and luxury items such as golf-ball-size gems, a mink tuxedo, and a fur-lined bathrobe. His real estate portfolio included homes in Texas and three in California neighborhoods. The American taxpayer and the Newport-Mesa Unified School District were very, very good to Stephen Wagner.

Writing checks to his own bogus businesses, Wagner siphoned money from several different school accounts, including cafeteria funds and those used to pay employee health care costs. A trusted employee for 21 years, he had risen from bookkeeping clerk to become the school district's chief financial officer. When he was taken into custody at his luxurious home his wife and four-year-old son looked on.

A long overdue audit revealed that Wagner had written dozens of school checks payable to himself and to businesses he owned. Twenty-five cashiers' checks totaling $920,625 were deducted from the district's health fund and were deposited in Wagner's personal bank accounts. "It makes me furious," said the mother of a 13-year-old student. "He stole a fortune from our schools and no one even noticed." Auditors discovered that interest income on the health plan was never recorded on the books.

Wagner also wrote checks for $175,300 to the Cobbler Express Corporation (a shoe repair store he owned) and wired a school check for $90,500 to a Florida jewelry company.

Despite his lawyer's ranting, Wagner was found guilty of diverting at least $3.5 million in school funds to his personal accounts between 1986 and 1992 and failing to disclose the income on his tax returns. For these horrendous crimes against the education system—the largest school embezzlement case in the state's history—Wagner was sentenced to a mere six years in prison and ordered to pay back the $3.5 million.

With credits earned for good behavior, Wagner may serve only two and a half years in prison. This means that he will serve approximately one day in prison for every $3840 he stole. The reality is that restitution will not be made; the school district will never be fully reimbursed. Money that could have been spent on scholarships, books, computers, teachers' salaries, and better security is gone forever. Authorities did freeze Wagner's properties, but the total assets equaled only a fraction of the stolen sums, and Wagner had been clever enough to file for bankruptcy a year before he was convicted.

Putting a Stop to Embezzling in Education

A great first step to reducing embezzling is to know the tactics that criminals utilize. Crooks can utilize hundreds of different varieties of simple scams to steal from 100 separate educational accounts. It is essential that the taxpayers' guardians audit each educational account *separately* (criminals use different techniques to steal from each specific account). Administrators need to familiarize themselves with double billing, ghost employees, phantom-purchasing, and the many other tactics white-collar criminals regularly use to steal $8 billion a year from education. You are less likely to be a victim if you are aware of these tactics.

Know what to look for. Embezzlers right now are stealing vast amounts of money from at least 20,000 schools and colleges in the United States. Although most employees are honest, a small percentage of any large group is likely to be greedy, conniving, and crooked. Entrusted with limited educational funds, today's administrator must tighten internal controls, take a closer look at the books, be attentive to details, insist on routine audits, and understand that embezzlers can be male or female, young or old, or "the nicest guy in the world." Educators found guilty of embezzlement have almost always been respected, well-liked individuals who were in positions of trust and authority and had easy access to the money.

Auditors have to remember to check the checks. Taking advantage of sloppy bookkeeping and lax internal controls, a high percentage of white-collar criminals forge checks to steal money from schools and colleges. Ask the right questions:

- Are the checks going to a bogus vendor, a phony company, or a nonexistent employee?
- Are the checks paying for construction that was not needed or overpriced, for services that were never performed, or for supplies that were never delivered?
- Are checks written to the school being deposited in questionable accounts? Who opened these accounts and who has access to them?
- Are checks payable to a company controlled by a school employee?
- Have the signatures on the checks been forged? To tighten controls, at least two signatures should be required to approve and sign checks.
- Are employee mailboxes secure? Many checks and other materials are stolen from mailboxes.

Do not allow anyone to pick up checks on behalf of other employees. Set limits on the amount of money each supervisor is allowed to approve, and hold that supervisor accountable for each check. Be suspicious if a large number of checks for small amounts are suddenly being written on a particular account. The checks that white-collar criminals use to steal money are often the same checks that lead to the offender's capture.

Dishonest employees steal millions of dollars each year by submitting false travel claims and by using a tactic called double billing. If auditors at every school and college specifically focused on the double-billing tactic, they would save U.S. taxpayers an estimated $28 million a year.

As the use of computers to perform administrative tasks becomes more common, computer-related crime becomes more widespread as well. Evaluating each computerized account separately, computer-literate educators need to think like a crook and ask, "How could a dishonest employee or an outside hacker manipulate the system to steal money?" Ask your employees and your campus experts, "What are the security weaknesses?" Ask administrators in other schools, "How have criminals at your school used computers to steal funds?" Facing up to the threat, administrators will need to limit access to the computerized accounts and implement a series of safeguards if they want to prevent theft and sabotage. It is important to understand that secret passwords do not guarantee computer security.

Act fast. Suspicions of fraud and embezzlement should be acted upon immediately so that alleged perpetrators cannot take advantage of statute of limitations laws. In 1994, a case against a former bookkeeper at the University of Southern California who was highly suspected of stealing $901,000 was thrown out of court when the statute of limitations ran out. The bookkeeper had been charged with stealing the money from donations, tuition, and endowment funds. A lawyer for the bookkeeper blamed the losses on "lax standards" and said that school officials knew about the disappearance of funds since 1989, "but never followed up on it." Taking advantage of slow-moving educational bureaucracies and of bureaucrats who choose to ignore theft, white-collar criminals have exploited the statute of limitations laws and escaped scot-free with billions of dollars.

Theft of Supplies and Equipment

Dishonest employees of educational establishments in the United States steal over $400 million in supplies and materials each year. This is $400 million the educational system in the United States cannot afford to lose. This is a $400 million loss that does not need to occur.

A former New York City school official admitted that he stole more than $600,000 by using fraudulent vouchers to purchase supplies. On April 17, 1995, a 63-year-old school administrator in Compton, California, pleaded guilty to approving four school district checks totaling $27,461 for supplies the district never received; the administrator had ordered supplies from two fictitious companies and pocketed the money. And in Pennsylvania, an assistant director of building and grounds for the Montgomery County school district was charged with stealing supplies worth $31,000 after police discovered school light bulbs, tools, tires, and electrical and plumbing materials in his two homes.

Although white-collar criminals use a variety of tactics to steal supplies and equipment from schools and colleges, they almost always succeed because of lax security, an informal credit system, inadequate supervision, antiquated inventory procedures, and either the ignorance or the negligence of their bosses.

On March 3, 1995, Joan Salvatore, a 53-year-old teacher

and administrator, pleaded guilty to stealing thousands of dollars from the New York City school system.

Utilizing the phantom-purchase scheme, a tactic that has been reported in all 50 of the United States, Ms. Salvatore worked out a deal with a man who owned an office supply company. She and the company owner created phony purchase orders to make it appear that the school system ordered thousands of dollars of supplies such as notebooks, staplers, scissors, calendars, pens, and pencils. Even though the supplies were never delivered, Ms. Salvatore would nonetheless certify full delivery to board accountants, who would pay the vendor in full. The vendor would then pay her a substantial cash kickback.

Authorities recovered about $100,000 from Ms. Salvatore and five other administrators involved in similar phantom-purchase schemes. "But, unfortunately, that sum represents less than one percent of the money pilfered each year by corrupt purchasers," said a New York City investigator.

School supplies are also stolen directly from warehouses by drivers and delivery personnel who have been hired to transport the merchandise to schools.

On April 25, 1995, two independent truck drivers were arrested in New York City and charged with conspiring with school warehouse employees to sell $32,000 worth of school supplies to private retail stores.

The drivers, who were under contract to the school system, reportedly paid bribes to warehouse workers to load extra cleaning materials, copier paper, light bulbs, rock salt, paper towels, and other supplies into their trucks. After delivering some of the supplies to schools throughout the city, the two drivers would sell the remaining stock to private store owners.

Conversations with investigators in 11 different states indicate that school supplies, paid for by taxpayers, are ending up in private stores nationwide. "We raided a party store in March '95," said a detective from Michigan, "and found tape recorders, copiers, lawn mowers, and writing materials that had been stolen from Detroit schools."

Computer Theft

Unable to manipulate manifests, vouchers, and purchase orders, tens of thousands of dishonest students and staff members have stolen large quantities of supplies and equipment the old-fashioned way—they simply snatched up their prize and carried it home. One of the most popular prizes in recent years has been the computer.

After a hidden camera caught an undergraduate student from Michigan University allegedly stealing computers, police raided his off-campus apartment and found another $10,000 worth of equipment.

Using the "stay behind" tactic, the 20-year-old chemical engineering major reportedly hid in a closet until the engineering laboratory closed. Then he unhooked the computers and other equipment, tossed them into a backpack, and nonchalantly walked out of the building. Police discovered a monitor in the student's bedroom that was hooked up to seven stolen disk drives, including one that had an incredible 760-megabyte storage capacity.

Unfortunately, the arrest of this one student did not end the computer theft problem at the University of Michigan. Quoting campus officials, Maryanne George of the *Detroit Free Press* found that the computer theft problem was much greater than most people realized: "University of Michigan police say that dozens of students, faculty, and staff members will steal nearly $400,000 worth of computer equipment from the University of Michigan this year."

It is not known exactly how much money is lost each year as a result of computer theft from high schools and colleges, but the sum is certainly in the tens of millions of dollars. A randomly selected sampling of just 30 colleges and universities revealed that their one-year losses due to computer theft alone totaled $1,839,000—an average of $61,300 per school.

The problem has become so serious that many insurance companies will not reimburse schools for theft unless the computers are bolted down, secured in a room with burglar alarms and security cameras.

Keeping an Eye on School Property

White-collar criminals routinely take advantage of poor security, informal credit systems, insufficient checks and balances, outdated inventory procedures, and either the ignorance or the compliance of educators. The theft of $400 million in supplies and equipment each year from U.S. schools and universities indicates that something is seriously wrong. It is a signal that the educational establishment should be held accountable for its funds and start educating itself about theft.

Administrators need to focus more attention on the many phantom-purchase schemes described in this section. They need to conduct surprise, in-depth inspections (a signed paper is *not* proof that supplies were needed or delivered), hold designated individuals accountable for equipment, and patch up the obvious security weaknesses.

Keepers of the purse need to scrutinize expenditures more closely, ask more specific questions, require item-by-item accounting, and be held accountable for the public's money.

Student-Aid Shenanigans

"You want to know how one-third of your financial-aid tax dollars is being spent?" a U.S. Department of Education official asked as he motioned toward the bathroom. "Then imagine the sound of a million flushing toilets."

The federal government, the American taxpayer, and the educational system in the United States have been losing at least $4 *billion* annually to student-aid shenanigans alone. Four billion tax dollars each year are being looted by dishonest administrators and students to purchase luxury vehicles and real estate, support $200-a-day crack cocaine habits, invest in personal and religious causes, and help themselves to million-dollar salaries. This is not fiction, or speculation or theory; it is fact.

Sadly, for every crook who is caught looting the financial aid coffers, nine others go scot-free. Fifty-three-year-old Dora Malfrici engaged in deception for a decade before becoming part of the 10 percent who get caught.

New York University

On December 3, 1992, Mrs. Malfrici, a retired New York University (NYU) financial aid administrator, pleaded guilty to stealing $4.1 million in university funds by collecting 1000 tuition-assistance checks she issued from 1982 to 1992 to nonexistent students and to students who were not entitled to any money.

Treating taxpayers' money like state lottery winnings, Mrs. Malfrici and her husband, Salvatore, spent a whopping $785,000 on expensive jewelry and $85,000 on Florida real estate and used the rest to buy stocks and to live the lifestyle of the rich and famous.

At the time of her arrest, the 35-year former employee of NYU had been retired for one year and had moved to Fort Myers, Florida, with her 60-year-old husband, who would later plead guilty to aiding in the thefts.

Mrs. Malfrici smiled confidently following her arraignment, adamantly proclaimed, "I never stole anything," and feigned befuddlement with the entire proceeding. But as the FBI subpoenaed more and more banks, witnesses, and university records, Mrs. Malfrici's demeanor suddenly turned sheepish and her sweet smile became a scowl. The rich woman who exuded absolute confidence and wore so much jewelry was now visibly scared.

The $4.1-million theft that went undetected for 10 years was discovered when the university switched to a computerized system that improved its method of cross-referencing financial records one month after Mrs. Malfrici retired. With the new system, NYU auditors noticed "irregularities" (a euphemism for "We've been robbed!") in the Tuition Assistance Program (TAP), a state-financed financial-aid program that assists needy students.

Mrs. Malfrici's job was to make sure that students who were entitled to funds received their checks. But Mrs. Malfrici was apparently confused about her job description. Investigators discovered that Mrs. Malfrici falsified documentation and had more than 1000 checks made out to students who were not entitled to the money. Those students never knew about the checks. In other cases, Mrs. Malfrici had checks made out to students who didn't exist.

The good news is that NYU got lucky with this case. A sharp-eyed auditor, a new computer program, and a team of tenacious, well-trained investigators were able to put a crooked couple in jail and return $4.1 million to the educational system. The bad news is that there are still thousands of dishonest men and women who, at this very moment, have both hands deep in the till.

The Pell Grant Fraud

Most of the $4 billion stolen annually from the many student-aid programs is siphoned from the U.S. government's Pell Grant program. The Pell Grant is the government's primary aid program for students after high school and provides $6.3 billion in grants annually to 4.4 million students who want to attend vocational schools, colleges, and universities.

Quoted in the *New York Times*, James B. Thomas, Jr., the Education Department's Inspector General, estimated that "several hundred million dollars" a year is being defrauded from the Pell Grant program alone. Responding to Thomas's estimate, Senator Sam Nunn, chairman of the Senate Permanent Subcommittee on Investigations, stated, "Based on what we've seen, if it's that amount we're fortunate."

Dishonest Administrators

Although dishonest students steal millions of dollars from the Pell Grant program each year, the most serious abuses are perpetrated by dishonest school administrators.

Tony Russell, the former assistant academic coordinator

for the University of Miami athletic department, pleaded guilty in 1994 to falsifying Pell Grant applications worth $220,000 and spending the money on a $200-a-day crack cocaine habit.

In a conversation with Dan Le Batard of the *Miami Herald*, a University of Miami football player explained that Russell approached him one evening and suggested he apply for a Pell Grant, reserved for needy students. The athlete told Russell that he wasn't eligible for the grant because his parents made too much money.

"Don't worry," the athlete remembers Russell saying. "Everybody is eligible."

Armed with a phony document, Russell conned scores of football players, swimmers, and tennis players into signing blank application forms. At one point, authorities would later learn, the line of athletes outside Russell's office door waiting for grant applications grew so long that extra chairs had to be placed in the hallway.

"I honestly believed the money I got was legal and aboveboard," said one 23-year-old recipient who drives a $40,000 automobile.

Many schools throughout the United States and Puerto Rico have fraudulently obtained millions of dollars in Pell grants. In 1987 the U.S. Department of Education began investigating Continental Training Service (CTS), a national trucking school chain based in Indianapolis that had received $117 million ($117,000,000!) in Pell funds. When it was discovered that CTS had falsified documentation to become eligible for Pell grants and was providing inadequate and limited training, the Education Department rode to the rescue and filed a lawsuit seeking $360 million in refunds and damages.

Utilizing a legal loophole that has been exploited by thousands of white-collar criminals, CTS protected itself by declaring bankruptcy. Consequently, after almost six years of costly litigation at taxpayers' expense, the government's $360 million lawsuit with CTS was settled in 1992 for a mere $50,000. One small step for education, one giant leap for crime.

Although some criminals still steal money the old-fashioned way—with a gun and a mask—the robber who stalks the educational system is more likely to rely on a toothy smile and a government-issued PIN (personal identification number).

More valuable than the goose that lays golden eggs, PINs are given to any school that is certified for a Pell Grant and can be used to obtain money much the way a bank customer uses a personal identification number at an automatic teller machine. The difference, of course, is that the Pell users are withdrawing taxpayers' money, not their own, and are playing with a balance of more than $6 billion.

When Gerardo Tirado Torres, owner of Advanced Business College in Puerto Rico, received his PIN, he probably raised his arms to the heavens and screamed, "What a world!"

Torres was later convicted of using his Pell Grant PIN to make at least seven illegal withdrawals totaling $3.3 million. In a front-page article for the *New York Times* on February 2, 1994, Michael Winerip reported that Torres used taxpayer money to buy several Mercedes-Benzes, a Volvo, a Peugeot, new businesses, and real estate. One shudders to think about what was being taught at the Advanced Business College.

Unfortunately, it gets worse. In a 1993 inquiry conducted by Senator Nunn's Senate Permanent Subcommittee on Investigations, it was charged that 20 Orthodox Jewish schools in New York City and one in Los Angeles had become so-called Pell mills, illegally enrolling thousands of students primarily to produce federal aid. Many of the students interviewed by the subcommittee admitted they attended classes only because they received a $200-a-semester stipend, an apparent kickback for providing the school with a Pell Grant. Pell money is typically paid directly to the school and the student is then given tuition credit.

The investigation found evidence that federal aid applications appeared to be forged and that many schools had received grants in the names of students who didn't attend the schools.

Bais Fruma, one of the Brooklyn schools, offered independent study courses with no classrooms, teachers, books, or supplies, and had collected $22.4 million in taxpayers' money. Of the 2000 students enrolled at Bais Fruma, an incredible 97 percent had somehow qualified for Pell grants. Investigators learned that some 530 families in the community surrounding Bais Fruma had at least two members getting Pell money at the school, and one family had nine members receiving grants.

Panelists also learned that the schools apparently siphoned off much of the student-aid revenue to bankroll the Orthodox Hasidic sects' religious operations in Israel and the United States.

On October 28, 1993, investigator David Buckley told the subcommittee that the schools transferred $800,000 of the grants to an affiliate and that additional funds were contributed to a $1.2-million mutual-fund investment. Alan Edelman, the subcommittee counsel, reported that bank and school records indicated that Bais Fruma used Pell money to pay off mortgages on buildings in Brooklyn and that the school's sponsor, the Munkacser' Hasidic movement, apparently funneled Pell grants to religious institutions which were ineligible for Federal Aid.

Although Bais Fruma was terminated from federal aid programs in 1994, complicated, drawn-out legal proceedings continue, and the case will not be fully resolved for years.

Trade schools, in recent years, have collected approximately 22 percent of all loan revenue and have been responsible for an estimated 30 percent of the fraud. About 750,000 students are currently attending trade schools in the United States.

The 1990 Senate hearings on federal student-aid abuses spotlighted the American Career Training Corporation (ACT), a Florida school that trained secretaries and travel agents and collected $46 million per year in federal loan money.

Students and employees of ACT testified that they believed that the primary purpose of the school was to generate federal student loan revenue.

The FBI began investigating ACT in 1990 and hauled away three truckloads of incriminating evidence. But since the Education Department cannot free up the staff to work on the case, it still flounders five years later, and the chances of the government recouping any money are becoming very slim.

Inspector General James B. Thomas, Jr., testified in 1993 that the 21-year-old Pell program attracted fraud because it was so easy for criminals to get away with it; he was quoted in the *Wall Street Journal* as saying that the $6.3 billion program "operates essentially on an honor system."

Of the 7400 schools certified for federal student-aid

programs in 1993, only 25 were audited by the inspector general's office. When a case is identified as high priority "it means we hope to get to it in the next year or so," said Thomas.

Naively based on trust, the loosely regulated federal student-aid program in the United States is a bureaucracy that invites criminals to steal $4 billion each year and then finds that there is no money to monitor the program, investigate the fraud, or prosecute the criminals.

"Perhaps they should give more money to the investigators and less to the crooks," said a 15-year-old high school student from Bethesda, Maryland.

Monitoring Student Aid

To prevent losses by the federal government, the American taxpayer, and the educational system in the United States of at least $4 *billion* annually ($4,000,000,000!) to student-aid and Pell Grant fraud, agencies charged with protecting the public's money need to audit all the educational establishments receiving taxpayer money. They need to aggressively prosecute and punish offenders and publicize all convictions.

Adopting a zero-tolerance attitude towards fraud, these agencies need to give more resources to the investigators, and less to the crooks, by asking the tough questions:

- Is the school really entitled to government student-aid funds?
- Is the school actually providing the services and training claimed?
- Has the school not padded its enrollment?
- Is the student receiving financial aid real?
- Is the recipient entitled to aid?

Dishonest administrators and school employees frequently make up fictitious students and pocket the tuition-assistance checks. Tens of thousands of students (real and fictitious) have been illegally enrolled in programs so that trade schools and colleges could produce federal aid. A high percentage of these students never even attended classes. Many of these institutions provide little or no training and exist solely to obtain taxpayer money.

The U.S. government has the power and the knowledge to protect the public's money. It only needs to take the steps to do so. The most important of these is that student-aid programs in the U.S. can no longer afford to be run on the honor system. The proper checks and balances must be put into place.

Student Loan Defaults

Close your eyes and try to visualize a huge pile of a million one-dollar bills. Pretend you are sitting on top of this mountain of green and you are gleefully throwing handfuls of money into the wind. Now try to visualize 14,000 piles of one million one-dollar bills. That's how much money the U.S. taxpayer and the U.S. economy *lost* during the past five years due to bad student loans.

During the five-year period from January 1991 to January 1996, deadbeat students defaulted on $14 *billion* in student loans. This devastating loss hurts the economy, hurts education, and hurts students who will need loans in the future.

Although some economists and sociologists offer teary-eyed excuses for the scofflaws, the vast majority of deadbeats could easily make payments if they chose to do so.

The formula is really very simple. The U.S. government agrees to loan a student some of the taxpayers' money so that the student can afford to attend school. Appreciating the opportunity this money represents, the student thanks the taxpayer for the loan and signs an agreement to pay back the money within a certain number of years. The student understands that the loan, ranging from a few hundred dollars to more than $275,000, is *not* a gift. The taxpayers worked for this money and they want it paid back.

But tens of thousands of students are rationalizing, without any apparent guilt, that it is okay to renege on the loan agreement. It's as if they are saying, "I got mine so to hell with society, to hell with the next generation, and to hell with the written agreement."

Some of the excuses and some of the reasoning for not paying back the student loans are both baffling and scary.

"I can't afford to pay $200 per month," said a 29-year-old computer programmer from New Jersey who made $36,000 in 1994. What he means, of course, is that it's easier and more fun to have a good time and buy things for himself than it is to pay back his $14,000 college loan. The man admitted that the thick gold chain around his neck, which he charged on MasterCard, cost nearly $2500 and that he typically spent "at least" $300 per month ($3600 each year) on recreation.

When asked if he made payments to MasterCard, the same man replied, "Oh yeah, if you don't it will ruin your credit."

Many employed debtors who can well afford to pay back their school loans feel "you are a sucker if you do" and blatantly refuse to pay a penny, "unless they come and get me."

A 33-year-old former student from Alaska, where up to 40 percent of student loans are in default, boasted that he once made $97,000 in eight months with an oil company, but has never made a single payment on his $17,000 school loan. "No one else does, why should I?" he said with an in-your-face attitude.

"I don't know what scares me more," said an employee of a California student-aid group charged with contacting debtors, "their lack of integrity or the illogical rationalizations they use to justify illegal behavior."

"Although many stereotype the typical scofflaw as an unemployed inner-city student," explained the same employee, "in California we are chasing over 600 medical professionals who owe an average of $40,000 apiece."

Nationwide more than 5000 doctors, dentists, chiropractors, optometrists, pharmacists, psychologists, and other health workers have defaulted on more than $228 million in government loans.

In 1993 the government decided to get tough and turned over the 5000 names to the Internal Revenue Service and the U.S. Justice Department for collection. Borrowers whose repayments were overdue suddenly found that they were barred from receiving reimbursement from the Medicaid and Medicare patients they treated.

Another "get tough" decision, applauded by most taxpayers, was the printing of the debtor's names and the amounts they owed in the *Federal Register,* a widely read federal publication that is frequently perused by the media. Prior to that the government respected the debtors' privacy and insisted that the loan recipients' names be kept confidential.

Embarrassed doctors who previously thumbed their noses at their debts suddenly began making payments. Defaulters' names and addresses and the names of the medical schools they attended are now published annually, a decision ordered by Congress.

Hundreds of millions of dollars in loans are also owed by former students who are currently working as lawyers, teachers, architects, and business owners. Like the deadbeats in the medical fields, the vast majority of these debtors have the means to pay back their loans but have simply chosen to spend the monthly payments on other priorities. And the primary reason hundreds of millions of dollars are still owed by deadbeat lawyers, teachers, architects, and business owners is because the government, state and federal, has not been creative or tough enough with the debtors.

The government is not to blame; the debtor is to blame. But if the government loans the public's money, it's the government's responsibility to collect.

Winning the Student Loan Standoff

The only answer is for the educational system and the U.S. government to get tough with the deadbeats and insist that they pay back the billions of dollars the taxpayers loaned to them.

At the very least, the names of deadbeats should be held up for public scrutiny. Credit bureaus should be notified and government benefits should be withheld until loans are repaid. The current attitude that "it costs too much to collect the money" sets an even costlier precedent. Coddling the deadbeats punishes not only the taxpayers but also students who will need student loan money in the future.

The Impostors

When 25-year-old Lon Grammer was arrested in his dormitory at Yale University on April 6, 1995, and charged with taking $61,475 in educational loans and scholarships under false pretenses, he was only two months away from earning a degree in political science.

Grammer had transferred to the prestigious Ivy League university two years earlier from Cuesta College in California. It was highly unusual for a student from a small community college in San Luis Obispo to be accepted by Yale, but Grammer's credentials were absolutely top-notch: a nearly perfect 3.9 college grade-point average, a high class rank, and laudatory recommendation letters from two college instructors and a dean.

The only problem was that Grammer was living a life of lies, and Yale had been duped. Every aspect of Grammer's academic record was a fraud. He submitted a falsified high school transcript, forged and inflated his community college grade-point average from C to A+, provided two glowing letters of recommendation from people who didn't exist, and forged a third recommendation from a college dean. He then accepted $41,475 in university and federal grants and nearly $20,000 in loans.

Grammer's ego led to his undoing. Apparently thinking his roommate would be impressed, Grammer boasted about getting into Yale with fake documents. The roommate, who was not impressed with fraud, contacted authorities and Grammer's elaborate scheme unraveled.

Yale, of course, is not the only Ivy League school to be duped by impostors. Princeton and Harvard have been conned by impostors on several occasions—once by the same man.

In 1989, 29-year-old James Arthur Hogue submitted a series of fake documents and convinced admissions officers, professors, coaches, and students at Princeton University that he was Alexi Indris-Santana, a 21-year-old self-educated cowboy who grew up on a commune, worked on the Western Plains with his horse Good Enough, and managed to score an impressive 1450 on his Scholastic Aptitude Test. Trying for the sympathy vote for good measure, the candidate falsely stated that his mother, a sculptress, was dying of leukemia in Switzerland and that his father had been killed in a car crash. He claimed that he educated himself by reading the great books.

"What an extraordinary and intriguing young man," the admissions officers at Princeton must have thought. "Let's give him a try."

After traveling to Princeton from Utah, "Indris-Santana" entered classes, participated in track, and during the next two years received thousands of dollars in financial aid from the U.S. government and the university.

But when Indris-Santana was a sophomore he fell victim to the realities that bring down most impostors—it's a small world and you can't fool all the people all the time. His true identity came to light when he was recognized at a track meet at Yale University in Connecticut. A Yale team member recognized him as the man who, at age 26, had masqueraded as a 16-year-old high school student in California. The Yale athlete told her coach about her discovery, the coach told a newspaper reporter, and the reporter discovered that Indris-Santana was actually James Hogue, wanted in Utah for parole violations.

On March 4, 1991, police arrested Hogue outside his geology lab at Princeton University. He had been unmasked.

Shocked students and administrators at Princeton learned that Hogue was a complete impostor who had been incarcerated in Utah for stealing $20,000 worth of tools and bicycles and had once pretended to be a Stanford University Ph.D. in bioengineering.

On October 23, 1992, Hogue was sentenced to nine months in prison and was ordered to repay the $22,000 in financial aid he bilked from Princeton. The judge ordered Hogue to begin his sentence immediately, but an appeals court agreed to let him finish his semester at an extension program in Massachusetts.

While finishing his semester in Massachusetts, Hogue, the perfect picture of prep, transferred his trickery to Harvard. Seeing a help wanted ad for a part-time cataloger at the Harvard Mineralogical Museum, Hogue conned the university into believing he was the perfect candidate.

During the next few months Hogue allegedly smuggled over $50,000 in gems, minerals, and equipment from the museum, finished his semester, and on December 18 returned to New Jersey to serve about four months of his original nine-month sentence at Mercer Correctional Institute. The curators at the Harvard Mineralogical Museum would not discover the theft until shortly before Hogue was released from prison in New Jersey.

Backtracking through museum employment records and acting on a tip, police in Massachusetts obtained a warrant and searched Hogue's Massachusetts apartment. They discovered $50,000 worth of gems, a stolen $10,000 microscope, and university-owned furniture.

On May 10, 1993, Hogue was released from prison and returned to Massachusetts. He was arrested by Massachusetts police on that same day and charged with the theft.

Majoring in deception, more than 1000 impostors con

their way into colleges and universities each year. Some assume a completely new identity and others keep their true names but falsify their qualifications.

Qualifications and credentials are enhanced by computer hackers who break in and change academic records, by forgers, and by school employees on the inside who accept bribes. A former registrar at Coolidge High School in Washington, D.C., was arrested January 7, 1994, and charged with taking money for forged student transcripts.

In dozens of documented cases, high school seniors have hired smart impostors to take the Scholastic Aptitude Test (SAT), the national college entrance exams, for them. Although no one knows the exact number of students who cheat on the SAT using a wide range of tactics, approximately 450 students are *caught* each year cheating on the exam. It is assumed that for every student who is caught cheating, several others are successful in their scam.

More than 125 impostors who have conned their way into colleges and universities in recent years are actually fugitives, hiding out from the law.

Students and teachers at Rend Lake College in Ina, Illinois, believed that Ricky Cummings, a transfer student from Los Angeles, was a polite, hard-working basketball player who only wanted to escape the chaos of the city in order to concentrate on his studies. They were naturally shocked when police arrested him for possession and distribution of cocaine. And they were even more shocked to learn that his real name was Stevie Stevenson, a fugitive wanted on charges of attempted murder, kidnapping, and armed robbery.

All is not always as it appears to be. In early 1995, Harvard University accepted a promising young woman originally from South Carolina who was about to graduate from a Cambridge, Massachusetts, high school. In her admissions application Gina Grant said she was an orphan, explaining that her father had died of cancer when she was 11 years old and that her mother had died in 1990 in an accident. However, Harvard was forced to withdraw the acceptance when they learned that the student had been accused of bludgeoning her mother to death with a lead crystal candlestick and had pleaded no contest to voluntary manslaughter.

Impostors in the educational environment are not always students; in hundreds of recorded cases they have been teachers.

In 1993, a 37-year-old woman with neither a college degree nor a teacher's certificate forged university transcripts and got a job teaching children at Westview Elementary School in Virginia. When her scam was discovered, the court ordered her to repay the money she had earned as a teacher.

On May 13, 1994, Gregory Motley, 32, pleaded guilty to using forged documents to land a teaching and coaching job at Near North High School in Chicago. Motley had been teaching without having earned a bachelor's degree or a teaching certificate.

In Phoenix, Arizona, Dailene Myers, a convicted thief and impostor, was removed from her job as principal of St. Mary's Elementary School after her educational credentials were found to be bogus. Myers, who reportedly embezzled $1500 from the school, was arrested again in 1995, this time for impersonating a doctor.

During the past decade, hundreds of teachers and professors are known to have lied about their degrees and qualifications, and dozens of educators have been arrested as fugitives.

In Nebraska, a university instructor in criminal justice who was married to the assistant dean of a state law school was arrested after being a fugitive for 11 years. The instructor had eight felony convictions and had escaped from prison.

On May 15, 1995, Dennis Taylor, a College of William and Mary dean and director of the Virginia Institute of Marine Science, resigned after admitting he had faked a doctor of science degree.

Rather than spend the money or the time to get a college degree, many teachers and professors have lied about their degrees, forged degrees, or ordered fake mail-order degrees from so-called diploma mills.

Armed with fake credentials and a gift of gab, thousands of impostors in our schools are costing the taxpayer millions of dollars and are making a mockery of education.

Tips for Fighting Back

- A great first step to reducing embezzling is to know the strategies that criminals use. You are less likely to be a victim if you are aware of the tactics.

- Administrators need to tighten internal controls, take a closer look at the books, be attentive to details, insist on routine audits, and understand that embezzlers can come in all shapes and sizes.

- Auditors have to remember to check the checks. Sloppy bookkeeping and lax internal controls allow a high percentage of white-collar criminals to forge checks.

- Do not allow anyone to pick up checks on behalf of another employee. Set limits on the amount of money each supervisor is allowed to approve, and hold that supervisor accountable for the check. Be suspicious if a large number of checks for small amounts are suddenly being written on a particular account.

- Watch out for double billing tactics.

- Guard computer files. Evaluate each computerized account separately, limit access to the computerized files, and implement a series of safeguards to prevent theft and sabotage.

- Keepers of the purse need to scrutinize expenditures more closely, ask more specific questions, require item-by-item accounting, and be held accountable for the public's money.

- The names of student loan deadbeats should be held up for public scrutiny. Credit bureaus should be notified and government benefits should be withheld until loans are repaid.

- Student-aid programs in the U.S. like the Pell Grant need to be taken off the honor system. The proper checks and balances must be put into place.

- Get involved; report criminal activities. Students and staff members have saved billions of dollars by reporting suspected criminal activities to the proper authorities.

In a random sampling of 200 embezzlements and other white-collar crimes at schools and colleges, nearly 70 percent of the perpetrators were caught because a lone tipster decided to get involved.

- Act fast. Suspicions of fraud and embezzlement should be acted upon immediately so that alleged perpetrators cannot take advantage of statute of limitations laws.

CHAPTER 2

The Medical Maelstrom

There's nothing quite like easy money. Attacking from every direction, an army of white-collar criminals is stealing $100 *billion* a year from the U.S. health-care system and rapidly bleeding the bureaucracy dry.

An ophthalmologist in California was sentenced to 16 months in jail and fined $686,000 after being convicted of submitting 687 false eye surgery bills to Medicare. He stole $1.1 million before being caught. In New York, the director of a methadone treatment center billed Medicaid for 1100 patients he never saw. He was sentenced to two to six years in prison for stealing $1.6 million. And in Maryland, a 42-year-old obstetrician/gynecologist got rich treating the poor by falsely claiming that he had delivered babies for 121 indigent women. He stole $115,646. The doctor's girl-friend told investigators that he seemed to enjoy the scheme and once stated, "This is the easiest money I ever made."

Medical Scams

The Drug Trade

Sadly, a lot of the fraud and abuse revolves around drugs.

Armed with pens and prescription pads, instead of pistols, thousands of medical professionals, including doctors, nurses, and pharmacists, are pushing drugs within the health-care system and profiting from the illicit drug trade.

Some are stealing drugs from Medicaid, the federal health-care program for welfare recipients, and others are ripping off Medicare, the health-care system for older adults.

In Baltimore, Maryland, on June 24, 1991, a 43-year-old geriatric and internal medicine specialist pleaded guilty to a drugs-for-sex Medicaid fraud case and was ordered to pay the U.S. government $385,000 in restitution. The doctor was providing 11 women who had histories of drug problems with narcotics and tranquilizers in exchange for sexual favors. Since Medicaid was billed for the office visits and narcotics, the taxpayers were unknowingly paying for the doctor's drug and sex parties.

Police have discovered many drug-trafficking conspiracies involving doctors, pharmacists, and patients. In one popular scam, a doctor prescribes drugs for a Medicaid beneficiary who he knows isn't ill or injured, and then bills Medicaid for the visit and the drugs. The patient then has the government-paid prescription filled by a pharmacist who is also involved in the swindle. After receiving the prescription, the patient sells the drug at 10 percent of its value to a person known as a diverter. The diverter, in turn, resells the drug back to the pharmacy or another person who then repackages it and sells it to the unsuspecting public.

Some pharmacists fill prescriptions with generic drugs

and bill Medicaid and Medicare for the more expensive brand-name product. In other cases, insurers have been charged multiple times for the same prescription.

The most common tactic, used by hundreds of dishonest pharmacists in 1995 alone, is to charge the government for prescriptions that were never ordered or filled.

On March 29, 1995, in York, Pennsylvania, police charged a 43-year-old pharmacist with defrauding Medicaid of $175,000. Using the names and medical assistance numbers of his customers and the physician license numbers of local doctors, the pharmacist submitted 1700 fraudulent claims for drugs that physicians never prescribed.

A pharmacist in Laurel, Maryland, was even greedier. On August 4, 1995, police charged the 30-year-old pharmacist and his 26-year-old wife with bilking Medicare out of $830,000. Like hundreds of other dishonest pharmacists across the country, the couple billed for prescriptions— thousands of prescriptions—that were never ordered or filled.

Faulty Equipment and Unnecessary Procedures

Thousands of white-collar criminals have gotten rich by selling faulty medical equipment or by ordering equipment that wasn't needed.

On August 24, 1995, in Boston, Massachusetts, three former executives of C. R. Bard Inc., one of the world's largest health-care products companies, were convicted of conspiring to conceal deadly flaws in artery catheters that had killed two people, and of using heart patients as human guinea pigs to test their product.

The convictions of the three Bard executives came two years after the company pleaded guilty to 391 fraud charges and paid the government a whopping $61 million in fines, a sum equal to the company's gross revenues from the 20,000 faulty catheters.

Although dealing in faulty or unnecessary medical equipment is bad, ordering unneeded operations can be even worse.

The harsh reality is that thousands of patients each year are conned into uncomfortable, expensive, and often life-threatening surgical procedures that are medically unnecessary.

In California, authorities charged a 41-year-old doctor with performing 30 unneeded surgeries—including cataract operations—on elderly patients, bilking Medicare out of millions of dollars. The doctor allegedly manipulated exams and tests to justify his actions, operated on patients who did not realize they were undergoing surgery, and reused disposable suture equipment and needles during operations.

Some doctors will treat patients for minor ailments but will charge insurers for a more serious condition. On May 5, 1995, in Falls Church, Virginia, Dr. Omar S. Zaki, 48, was sentenced to 51 months in prison for inflated billing practices that cheated insurers out of $2 million. He told insurers he was treating his patients for serious heart problems when in fact they were only suffering from sunburn or insect bites.

Phantom Patients

Other dishonest doctors will simply eliminate the middleman and bill for patients they never saw. On April 27, 1995, in Miami, Florida, a cosmetic surgeon who was already serving a five-year sentence for letting a patient bleed to death was sentenced to an additional 26 months for defrauding Medicare out of $441,000.

The doctor had billed Medicare for scores of patients he never saw and signed Medicare forms for several medical supply companies that charged Medicare for unnecessary equipment the patients didn't need or want.

One of the most surprising and expensive assaults on the health-care industry in recent years has been launched by the mental-health community.

Under the lofty guise of helping others, hundreds of dishonest psychologists and other mental-health professionals have faked diagnoses, kept patients longer than was necessary, and billed for patients they either never saw or saw only for a couple of minutes.

Rejecting his insanity defense as ludicrous, a jury in Newton, Massachusetts, convicted psychiatrist Richard Skodnek on August 1, 1995, of fraudulently billing Medicare and private insurers $500,000 for patients he never treated. Dr. Skodnek routinely made up diagnoses for real "patients" he had never seen and billed insurers for the nonexistent sessions. Many of those who were unknowingly labeled with severe psychological problems naturally worry that the false information will turn up in an insurance database and come back to haunt them.

Several companies specializing in mental-health concerns appear to be much more interested in making money than with helping their clients. In fact, many are making money at the expense of their patients' well-being.

On June 29, 1994, the National Medical Enterprises (NME), a national chain of psychiatric hospitals, agreed to pay an unprecedented $379 million in fines and penalties to settle federal charges that it provided unnecessary treatment to tens of thousands of patients to illegally collect insurance money.

"I kept telling everybody that's what they were doing," said a former patient who was being treated for insomnia, "but nobody would listen."

Using fake diagnoses, unnecessary medical treatments, and false billings, NME stole over $100 million from the federal insurance programs.

Suffering from an epidemic of white-collar crime, the medical profession in the United States is hemorrhaging from embezzlement and fraud.

Fraudulent Lab Tests

In the fall of 1993, in Washington, D.C., the Justice Department announced that two of the nation's largest blood testing laboratories paid $39.8 million to settle government charges that they made false blood-test claims to Medicare and manipulated doctors so that they would order unnecessary tests.

Although the $39.8 million restitution payment was certainly a victory for the Justice Department and a benefit to the U.S. taxpayer, this case represents only a very tiny portion of the problem.

The sad reality is that hundreds of medical labs across the country have charged billions of dollars for needless and fraudulent tests. And there are almost as many financial scams as there are labs.

Exposing Medical Scams

Don't be afraid to blow the whistle on white-collar crime in the medical world. In a review of 110 solved criminal cases involving the health-care industry, exactly 80 percent of the perpetrators were caught because a coworker, patient, or uninvolved taxpayer became aware of an offense, got angry, and reported the crime to the proper authorities. If you would report a bank robbery that you witnessed, then you should report a criminal who is stealing money from the health-care industry.

The money that's stolen from this industry is money that cannot be used for cancer, AIDS, or heart research. Less money means that more people will suffer or die. When money is pilfered from the health-care industry we all have to work a little harder and pay more taxes. There is less money for salaries, new equipment, training, and scholarships. The arrest of one white-collar criminal usually leads to the arrest of several more offenders.

At this very moment there are more than 300,000 honest health-care workers and patients who have intimate knowledge or strong suspicions of a white-collar crime. If all these people got angry and reported their suspicions to the police, the health-care system in the U.S. would save at least $50 billion.

The Embezzlers

Saying that he wanted to leave a legacy for his family, Roy R. Creech, a 60-year-old administrator with the Garwyn Medical Group in Maryland, embezzled $619,000. Needing to support her gambling habit, Sonia Lipton, a 60-year-old payroll clerk for St. Christopher's Hospital for Children in Philadelphia, embezzled $900,000. Hungering for all the nice things money could buy, Sherron Annette Hanna, a 52-year-old bookkeeper for an Arizona doctor, admitted that she made false computer entries and embezzled $436,000.

Each year in the United States, trusted employees embezzle hundreds of millions of dollars from hospitals, clinics, and private medical facilities.

Exploiting their special access and the trust bestowed on them, dishonest insiders use a wide range of deceptive techniques to steal.

Sonia Lipton, the payroll clerk who stole $900,000 from St. Christopher's Hospital for Children, forged signatures of hospital employees, mostly nurses, on checks that were not picked up on time. When the employees eventually asked for their checks, Lipton would reissue a new one. She also issued phony bonus checks in the names of employees and then cashed them herself.

Raymond Greene, a 33-year-old mailroom supervisor at Pennsylvania Hospital, devised a scheme that allowed him to embezzle $373,000.

Every day for six years, Greene went to the post office, purchased a five-dollar book of stamps, and asked the clerk to provide him with several receipts that added up to the five-dollar purchase price instead of just one receipt.

He would then alter each receipt to show a larger purchase price for the stamps and would get reimbursed by the hospital.

Apparently, nobody ever asked why Greene, who had access to the hospital's postage meter, always took time off to walk to the post office. Nobody was curious as to why he would buy stamps in small amounts, instead of buying in bulk. Nobody asked why he would turn in 5, 10, or 20 receipts a day for reimbursement, instead of just one receipt.

Greene, who was finally caught and convicted in 1991,

was sentenced to 10 to 23 months in prison and ordered to pay Pennsylvania Hospital $300,000 in restitution.

Dishonest employees who have the authority to transfer funds electronically can be especially dangerous.

On September 1, 1993, a judge in Fairfax, Virginia, froze the assets of an accountant and his wife, and of several companies linked to the accountant, in response to a multimillion-dollar lawsuit brought against him by a group of physicians. The physicians' group alleged that its longtime accountant had electronically transferred $13 million of their money into his own accounts. Confronted with the evidence, the accountant returned most of the money, but the doctors were still out $2.5 million.

The theft of more than $1 million from St. Francis Hospital and Health Center in Blue Island, Illinois, was also the result of an illegal and unauthorized money transfer. In that case, the investigation by FBI agents and hospital officials focused on a disgruntled, high-ranking financial officer.

Federal law requires financial institutions to disclose money transfers of $10,000 or more to the Justice Department. When it was noticed that more than $1 million had been transferred from St. Francis Hospital to a private account during a three-month period, authorities started asking questions. The financial officer was fired and prosecuted.

Many insider embezzlements involve the collusion of an outsider.

At Hahnemann University Hospital in Philadelphia, a fiscal officer was found to have disbursed $260,384 to an outside accomplice who provided no services to the hospital. The fiscal officer would write checks to the "ghost" vendor and then the two men would share the money.

One of the largest embezzlements involving insider and outsider collusion occurred at Cooper Hospital–University Medical Center in Camden, New Jersey.

On July 20, 1994, the hospital's executive vice president, the hospital's controller, and an outside vendor pleaded guilty to embezzling $3.8 million by using a fraudulent purchasing scheme.

The outside vendor, who owned a billing company, would send phony bills to the hospital for goods and services that the hospital never received. When the bills arrived at the hospital the executive vice president and the controller would approve the payments. The vendor and the two hospital executives would then split the spoils.

Embezzlements from medical facilities frequently involve checks.

At Liberty Medical Center in Baltimore two female employees pleaded guilty to embezzling $41,625. The women sent bogus patient-refund checks to friends who cashed the checks and returned most of the money to the employees.

Patricia L. Burnam, a 56-year-old employee of the Fairfax Hematology-Oncology Associates in Virginia, is thought to have stolen more than $110,000 by writing mountains of so-called business checks for personal profit. It is believed that Burnam would write a check for personal use but would log it into the system as a legitimate business expense.

Ever vigilant to the *outside* threat, many medical facilities turn a jaundiced eye to strangers while waving a cheery "good night" to the trusted, longtime employee who walks out the front door with pockets stuffed with cash.

Turning In the Embezzlers

Embezzlers are bleeding the medical industry dry. Treating the health-care system like a racketeering enterprise, more than 60,000 employees at all levels have embezzled and stolen sums ranging from $1000 to hundreds of millions of dollars. Stopping the bleeding will require a three-step operation:

1. Employees will have to come to grips with the dishonesty and criminality of some of their fellow employees;
2. Administrators will have to become knowledgeable regarding the embezzlers' tactics and implement tighter controls; and
3. The criminal justice system needs to adopt a zero-tolerance motto and consistently come down hard— very hard—on offenders.

In addition to stiffer fines and harsher prison terms, would-be white-collar criminals need to know that they could also be sentenced to shame and humiliation. Publicizing white-collar offenses in the newspapers and on television is one of the most effective deterrents. Employees who know that their deeds will be scrutinized by their colleagues and patients will be motivated to think before they steal. When crimes are hushed up and handled in-house, the deterrent value is significantly diminished.

Taxicabs and Ambulances: Taking Us for a Ride

Taxicabs

Taxicab drivers, in many cases, are taking Medicaid for a ride and U.S. taxpayers to the cleaners.

Medicaid, the health-care program for the poor, will pay $1.10 a mile for a taxi if a patient needs a ride to the doctor, job training, drug rehab, or other social services.

But scores of cab companies are getting rich by pretending to transport the poor.

In one case, reported by the *Miami Herald*, a West Palm Beach operator with just one licensed cab collected $295,900 by claiming he had driven Medicaid patients 269,000 miles in less than two months.

As the *Herald* pointed out, the cab would have had to have been rolling with a Medicaid passenger 24 hours a day, seven days a week, at 177 miles per hour to cover that much mileage.

Although much of the damage is already done—the horse is out of the barn—federal and state investigators are starting to crack down on taxi fraud.

In 1985 a driver from Allstars Taxi in Miami was charged with theft, forgery, and fraud. He allegedly billed Medicaid $576,794 for taxi rides that never occurred. In another case, the owner of United Taxi in Miami was accused of stealing $377,681 from Medicaid.

When a Medicaid recipient needs a ride, he or she shows a Medicaid card to a taxi driver, who records the passenger's identification number on a voucher. The driver then jots down the number of miles traveled and has the passenger sign the voucher. The voucher is then submitted to Medicaid for reimbursement.

But dishonest taxi drivers have figured out many ways to cheat the system.

Some drivers pay recipients to sign several blank vouchers. Charging for rides that never occurred, some drivers forge signatures and use the Medicaid identification numbers they obtained from previous customers. Others simply pad the number of miles traveled. "Add a zero to a three-mile trip and suddenly you got a thirty-mile trip," explained a driver in New York.

Medicaid recipients can also cheat on their taxi privileges. Riders sometimes claim they are taking a taxi to see a doctor when, in fact, they are going to a casino or liquor store in the same neighborhood. And sometimes Medicaid recipients loan or rent their cards to others.

In 1994, Medicaid paid $29 million for taxi rides in Florida alone.

Ambulance Services

On January 20, 1995, in Pennsylvania, a judge sentenced Mindi Rubin Raggi, who operated the Greater Philadelphia Ambulance Service, to 27 months in prison and fined her $50,000 for cheating Medicare and Medicaid out of $2.5 million. Raggi, a 39-year-old mother with three children, fraudulently claimed that her company was providing ambulance transportation for Medicare and Medicaid patients. The scheme was successful from 1986 until the company closed in 1991. Raggi was allowed to remain free pending appeal.

In Sunbury, Pennsylvania, on March 23, 1995, David Wertz, 59, the absentee owner of the defunct Elite Ambulance Service Inc., was charged with billing Medicare for $1.8 million in false claims. Wertz's scam had successfully bilked Medicare from April 1989 to March 1992.

On September 19, 1995, on Long Island, New York, William Eisenhauer, 51, owner of Metro Med Ambulette Inc., was charged with bilking Medicaid out of $442,000 by billing for 9000 fake ambulance rides. State Attorney General Dennis C. Vacco charged that in 43 cases Metro Med Ambulette claimed to have transported people who couldn't possibly have requested the service; they were dead.

Charged with cheating Medicare and Medicaid out of a total of $4,742,000, Raggi, Wertz, and Eisenhauer are only three of hundreds of men and women who have been accused of cheating the U.S. government by billing for fraudulent ambulance services.

Dishonest ambulance company owners and employees use many different tactics to milk the system.

Many companies have cheerfully provided elderly citizens with free rides to grocery stores, bingo games, churches, and synagogues and then billed Medicare, claiming the transportation was for medical reasons.

Many ambulance companies were found to be using vans and cars for transporting patients although they billed for ambulance services.

In scores of cases, ambulance companies have transported multiple patients but charged Medicare for separate transports. A company that regularly transported eight wheelchair patients simultaneously, three more than the vehicle was designed to carry, always billed Medicare for eight separate trips.

Ambulance companies are frequently authorized to transport a patient five to ten times per month. Many companies will bill Medicare for the five or ten trips per month even if the client canceled all the appointments.

The most popular and profitable scheme involving ambulance services has been the transportation of phantom patients. In thousands of known cases, the ambulance sat in a garage while Medicare and Medicaid were paying for patients who didn't exist.

Nationwide, hundreds of thousands of phony and fraudulent ambulance rides have cost taxpayers over $200 million during the past decade alone.

Some Extraordinary Cases

Miguel Recarey

In 1970, it behooved Miguel Recarey to renounce his Cuban citizenship and become a citizen of the United States. In 1988, it behooved Recarey—by then a millionaire many times over and an accused Medicare swindler—to renounce his American citizenship and become a citizen of Spain.

A rags-to-riches success story, Miguel Recarey started International Medical Centers (IMC) with one clinic in Miami, Florida, during the late 1970s. By 1986, IMC had thousands of subscribers, was considered one of the biggest health maintenance organizations (HMOs) in the nation, and was receiving $360 million a year—almost $1 million per day—from the U.S. government Medicare system.

But in 1987, amid allegations of forged HMO enrollments, phony billings, bribes to union officials, bugged offices, and other crimes, Recarey's clinics collapsed.

Under indictment, Recarey fled the United States to Venezuela. That's when investigators discovered the really bad news: IMC owed $230 million in unpaid claims, leaving patients and taxpayers in the lurch. Adding insult to injury, government regulators also discovered that Recarey had allegedly given a lawyer $355,000 in Medicare money (i.e., taxpayers' money), to finance his defense.

Curiously, the U.S. government made it extremely easy for Recarey to leave the country. Even though he was under indictment, a federal magistrate didn't impose any travel restrictions and the State Department graciously issued passports for his children. In August 1987, the Internal Revenue Service expedited Recarey's corporate income-tax refund of $2.2 million. Added to the Medicare money he allegedly embezzled, the $2.2 million income-tax refund provided Recarey with a comfortable life as a fugitive and certainly helped him to avoid capture.

Using phony passports and bribing foreign officials, Recarey proved to be an elusive fugitive. Not wanting to leave a paper trail, he didn't use credit cards and didn't list a telephone number or register a car in his own name.

In 1988, after spending a year in an exclusive suburb of Caracas, Recarey moved to Spain where he divorced his first wife, married a Spanish woman, and became a citizen.

On February 14, 1995, a top Spanish court ruled unanimously against the U.S. request for extradition.

Miguel Recarey, who had played the Medicare system like a game of Monopoly®, had collected a fortune, moved past jail, and won the game. He was home free.

The Bramson Bunch

A Maryland woman died after her podiatrist misdiagnosed her cancer. Her family sued the podiatrist's insurer and won a $600,000 malpractice settlement. But after winning the long and stressful court battle the family was unable to collect the money from the insurer. In Cleveland, a man who lost his leg because of medical negligence won a $450,000 malpractice suit. He will probably never see a penny of the much-needed money. A third patient sued two doctors for malpractice after she too lost a leg due to negligence. She won a $300,000 settlement but, like the others, has been unable to collect the money.

These three patients and at least 900 other people were all victimized by the Bramson bunch, a family of lawyers and medical professionals who stole $10 million and skipped the country.

On February 14, 1994, in Baltimore, Maryland, Norman Bramson, a 71-year-old optometrist, businessman, and con artist, was sentenced to 33 months in prison for his part in an international malpractice insurance scheme that fleeced millions of dollars from doctors and patients in the United States.

Bramson and his two sons, Martin and Leonard, both trained as lawyers, set up a web of 50 companies that sold bogus medical malpractice insurance policies to doctors.

The venture was extremely profitable for the Bramsons because the huge premiums paid by doctors were not applied to insurance; $10 million was pocketed directly or laundered through 240 banks in Europe, Canada, and the Caribbean.

When doctors made claims on the bogus policies, the Bramsons simply closed down that particular insurance company and opened up a new company under a different name.

Leonard Bramson, who launched his criminal career while still in law school, pleaded guilty to the scheme in 1992 and agreed to help authorities find his brother and father, who were both fugitives.

In early 1995, Martin Bramson, 49, who had eluded Interpol and FBI agents since 1991, was finally arrested and incarcerated in the tiny European nation of Liechtenstein.

But the 1936 extradition treaty between Liechtenstein and the United States, which covers only violent criminals, has no provisions for white-collar criminals. Martin Bramson will probably be released and will continue to spend his victims' money.

Akiyoshi Yamada

A financial wizard who attended Harvard Business School, Akiyoshi Yamada is charged with stealing $120 million from Medicare.

Considered to be among the nation's top three Medicare swindles, Yamada's criminal enterprise, which was the subject of investigations by ABC's *Primetime* and the *Miami Herald,* consisted of a massive network of Florida Medicare mills that recruited patients, faked diagnoses, paid kickbacks, and charged for medical services never rendered.

The son of a wealthy Japanese industrialist, Yamada, an exercise fanatic, is tall, lean, charming, and well educated. He is also no stranger to white-collar crime. In 1969 he convinced an eye doctor to let him handle the doctor's $1.4-million blue-chip portfolio. Yamada, who was 26 years old at the time, engaged in fraudulent stock manipulations and lost $1 million of the doctor's money.

Yamada then teamed up with John Peter Galanis, who once bilked investors out of $150 million in a real-estate swindle, and convinced 25 wealthy clients to invest $50,000 apiece in a company called Takara Partners.

Yamada and Galanis used the investors' money to bankroll stock scams and camouflaged their theft with glowing financial reports produced by bribed accountants. The Yamada/Galanis partnership ended in bankruptcy, and both served short prison terms after pleading guilty to fraud.

Always willing to try a new angle, Yamada pleaded guilty to forging a signature on a $75,000 cashier's check in 1980. In 1981 he violated his probation by consorting with a convicted felon. In 1987 he pleaded guilty to charges that he helped to run up the price of publicly traded stock in a medical company.

Freed on bond, Yamada moved to Miami in 1988 and began eyeing what would turn out to be his most lucrative criminal enterprise: the exploitation of the U.S. government Medicare system.

To a man like Yamada the easily manipulated Medicare bureaucracy offered endless possibilities for illicit profit. Medicare was a sitting duck.

Known for associating with notorious swindlers like Robert Vesco, who fled the country during President Nixon's administration, Yamada soon teamed up with Ismael Felipe Arnaiz, a convicted drug smuggler who was living in a prison halfway house in Miami. Yamada also began using the name Steve White.

Putting their criminal minds and organizational talents together, Yamada and Arnaiz engineered a massive Medicare fraud scheme consisting of 51 clinics, billing services, and patient transportation companies.

The crooked duo paid recruiters up to $300 for every patient they brought to a clinic. The professional patients, who were paid about $50 for each clinic visit, were told to fork over their Medicare cards and were coached to describe specific phony symptoms to a cadre of phony and real doctors, so that Medicare could be billed the maximum amount. The patients filled out their alleged medical histories and were told to sign blank forms which would be used to bill Medicare.

Making sure all his employees were happy, Yamada paid

crooked doctors $100 every time they signed a phony medical form used to justify the bogus Medicare bills.

During just one month, the FBI discovered, Yamada's recruiters bused nearly 700 phony patients to a single clinic.

Exploiting a system that was ripe with criminal opportunity, Yamada's corrupt organization ordered unnecessary tests and medical equipment, inflated claims, lied about illnesses, and victimized hundreds of thousands of future patients who, because of lack of funds, will be denied adequate medical care.

The Medical Masquerade

Medical school is expensive, difficult, and time consuming. So why bother? That's the reasoning of more than 1250 men and women who are known to have impersonated doctors and other medical professionals during the past seven years.

Masquerading as medical personnel, different criminals commit different types of crimes.

On January 7, 1989, in Manhattan, New York, Steven Smith, a 23-year-old homeless man, donned a doctor's lab coat, put a stethoscope around his neck, and then wandered, unchallenged, through the halls at Bellevue Hospital Center. Before departing the hospital he raped, robbed, and murdered Dr. Kathryn Hinnant, who was five months pregnant. Dr. Hinnant, 33, had been working in her office when the attack occurred.

A high percentage of the medical impersonators, however, are white-collar criminals who want to line their pockets and increase their status.

William J. Lott, 50, who preferred the name Dr. John R. Morrison, pretended to be a psychotherapist and charged

Medicaid $260,000 before being caught. Denny Pitts, 37, who masqueraded as "Dr. Ramos," obtained $50,000 worth of codeine and other drugs from the Department of Public Aid and sold his stash on the street. Abdul Jaleel Wahab, a former hospital clerk, added "M.D." to his name, claimed to perform physicals in patients' homes, and cheated Medicare out of $1.4 million.

Scores of white-collar criminals have doctored diplomas and résumés in order to land high-paying positions in the medical industry.

After a nationwide search that involved interviews with 50 candidates, health officials in Maryland unanimously selected Haroon R. Ansari, 33, to be the new $73,481-a-year director of the Crownsville Hospital Center, a facility that treats mentally ill patients.

Ansari claimed excellent academic credentials, including a doctorate in educational psychology from Michigan State University and master's degrees from Michigan State and Western Michigan University. And as the former deputy director of the Illinois Mental Health Administration, he appeared to have unique administrative experience as well.

But like hundreds of other professionals in the medical industry, Ansari turned out to be an impostor and a fraud.

The man selected to run the 253-bed hospital and oversee a $24-million budget did not have any of the degrees or any of the experience he had claimed on his résumé.

After running the hospital for nearly one year and collecting $63,000 in salary, the impostor was ordered to turn in his state car and resign.

The author has recorded over 200 cases in which unqualified and untrained impostors actually performed surgeries and other medical procedures before being unmasked.

Infamous con artist William Douglas Street, whose life as an impostor was depicted in the award-winning film *Chameleon Street*, once posed as a University of Michigan medical student and performed 36 hysterectomies at a Chicago hospital.

Self-described as the Great Impostor, Street, who has been in and out of prison and never graduated from high school, has been employed as a doctor, a lawyer, and a social worker.

Frank Abagnale, another infamous con artist, also pretended to be a doctor.

In his book *Catch Me If You Can*, Abagnale describes how he obtained fraudulent medical degrees and got hired as a pediatrician and night supervisor at a big city hospital. He had never gone to college and couldn't stand the sight of blood, but survived by ordering the interns and nurses to handle all the emergencies.

On one occasion a nurse summoned "Dr. Abagnale" to attend to a blue baby.

"Oddly enough, in the eleven months I'd posed as a doctor, I'd never heard the term *blue baby*," he says.

Thinking that the nurse must be joking, Abagnale reportedly responded, "I'll be right along, but first I've got to check the green baby in 609." He then stepped around the corner, consulted his medical dictionary, and discovered that a blue baby is one suffering from cyanosis, or lack of oxygen in the blood, usually due to a congenital heart defect.

"I took off for room 608, and was relieved to find one of my interns had bailed me out again," he recalls.

The interns at the hospital reportedly liked "Dr. Abagnale" because he treated them "like real doctors" and gave them free rein to practice medicine.

The 1250 impostors who have pretended to be doctors and nurses during the past seven years clearly illustrate that "All is not always as it appears to be."

Foiling Impersonators

Donning stethoscopes, scrubs, and white lab coats, many street criminals masquerade as medical personnel in order to gain access to hospitals and clinics. Once inside, these criminals typically steal drugs and equipment and commit robberies and other crimes.

Before hiring a new employee, the smart administrator will check bona fides, get certified confirmation of degrees and work experience, ask in-depth questions, and obtain a certificate of good standing from the disciplinary agency where the applicant worked. In terms of money and lives, medical impersonators are a huge liability.

A red-faced executive headhunter confided that the gentleman he recommended to be a hospital administrator "sure looked good on paper." But the gentleman whose résumé looked so good was actually a wanted ex-convict who had never graduated from or even attended college. (He did have some relevant work experience, however: He had worked in the prison infirmary.) Other white-collar criminals have pretended to be doctors and nurses so that they could order drugs (which they would then sell on the street) or charge Medicaid and Medicare for nonexistent patients.

The most dangerous impersonator is the unqualified, uneducated individual who actually gains employment as a doctor or nurse. "Hey, being a doctor for five months sure paid better than my construction job," one impostor quipped. Anyone can get a stethoscope, scrub suit, or white lab coat. And phony IDs, diplomas, and résumés are about as common as colds.

Tips for Fighting Back

- Blow the whistle on white-collar crime in the medical world. If you would report a bank robbery that you witnessed, then you should report a criminal who you know is stealing money from the health-care industry.

- Support ethics training. In response to the increasing conflict between medicine as an art and a profession and medicine as a business, many medical schools and employee training programs are making ethics courses mandatory. This is an important step in the right direction. A perusal of hundreds of thousands of separate cases illustrates that unethical health-care workers have committed every conceivable white-collar offense, including tax evasion, insurance fraud, check forgery, research and grant fraud, money laundering, and embezzlement. Injecting a return of ethics into a sick system, we need to remember that the practice of medicine is a much higher calling than just financial gain.

- Before hiring a new employee, administrators need to check bona fides, get certified confirmation of degrees and work experience, check with previous employers, ask probing questions, and verify professional references.

- In addition to fines and prison terms, would-be white-collar criminals need to know that they could also be sentenced to the stigma of public humiliation. Publicizing white-collar offenses in the newspapers and on television is very effective. Employees need to know that their misdeeds will be scrutinized by their colleagues and patients.

- The elimination of drug and alcohol abuse in the medical environment would probably reduce all types of medical employee crime by 70 to 90 percent. In a random sampling of 150 employees who committed white-collar offenses in the medical environment, 79 were believed to have serious drug and alcohol problems. Substance abuse among employees in the medical environment is as high as or higher than in the general population. Part of the problem is easy access to the drugs. All abusers should be confronted, counseled to seek help, and provided with any personal and professional support that is available. However, the abuser should also be reminded that both the hospital and the employee will be held liable for unprofessional or criminal behavior.

CHAPTER 3

Dishonest Lawyers

"Nobody can break the law like a lawyer," said a soon-to-retire federal officer who is himself a lawyer. "And the problem is that a hundred dishonest lawyers know a hundred different ways to steal."

There are almost 900,000 lawyers in the United States today. The vast majority of these lawyers apparently are honest and law-abiding.

But it is not true, as many in the legal profession would like people to believe, that the number of bad and corrupt lawyers represents less than one percent of the total. Such low estimates are absurd.

In reality, at least 17 percent of U.S. lawyers, or about 153,000 members of the bar, have at some time in their careers committed worse crimes than most of the criminals they have met in court. And if the number of lawyers who use slick and unethical tricks to get a guilty client off the hook was added in, the percentage would be dramatically higher than 17 percent.

Since many corrupt lawyers have cheated hundreds and even thousands of clients, there are at least 20 million citizens alive today who have been criminally victimized by a lawyer.

Plundering and pilfering every conceivable financial account, including trust funds, wills, pensions, and escrow accounts, dishonest lawyers in the United States pocket more than $14 billion annually.

Many lawyers take advantage of the most vulnerable citizens—the mentally and physically disabled, the poor, the uneducated, and the elderly.

New York lawyer Steven J. Romer, 55, was sentenced to prison for stealing $7 million from four clients including an orphan who was left destitute after losing her entire $740,000 inheritance. On October 18, 1994, lawyer Lawrence W. Shavers of Baltimore, Maryland, pleaded guilty to stealing more than $90,000 from a life insurance policy and other accounts belonging to a young boy whose mother had been brutally murdered. In Chicago, Illinois, lawyer Michael L. Cochran was disbarred for stealing $35,000 from the estate of a mentally disabled woman. And in New York, lawyer Melvyn Altman was charged with stealing $921,000, which included $206,400 from the bank account of a man who was declared mentally incompetent by the courts.

Any account with money has proven to be fair game for dishonest lawyers.

Abusing the Power of Attorney

Hundreds of lawyers are known to have exploited power of attorney authorizations to their criminal advantage.

A power of attorney is a legal document that authorizes one person (a lawyer, friend, or family member) to act as an agent for another in a wide range of financial and legal functions. Giving power of attorney to a dishonest lawyer is like giving a burglar the combination to one's safe.

In one case, a 74-year-old woman signed a power of attorney agreement with her son-in-law, a real estate lawyer, and gave him almost carte blanche permission to invest a $312,000 fund in a commercial real estate deal if he located a sound investment.

"I trusted him," she said. "He was my daughter's husband."

Unbeknownst to the woman, her daughter and son-in-law were having marital problems. The lawyer divorced his wife in order to start a new life with his mistress. Six months later, when the woman decided to look in on her $312,000 real estate deal, she discovered that the money had been invested in the lawyer's name, not hers.

Due to the wording of the power of attorney agreement, the judge politely concluded "in ten pages of legal mumbo jumbo" that "I didn't have a legal leg to stand on," the woman said. The lawyer kept the money without guilt.

In another case, the Texas Supreme Court barred attorney Donald E. Kilpatrick from practicing law because he had induced a brain-damaged, mentally incompetent man to sign a power of attorney agreement, even though the man's wife had already been appointed his guardian.

Kilpatrick demanded that the injured man's family pay him $277,000 to relinquish his so-called contract. In censoring Kilpatrick the jurists noted that he had violated ethical practices when he visited the man in his hospital room to obtain employment.

Cheating the Elderly and Disadvantaged

Dishonest lawyers target the elderly more than any other group. Anyone who peruses a computer printout of cases in which the elderly have been swindled by lawyers—tens of thousands of incidents—cannot help but feel a bit cynical about lawyers in general.

On October 22, 1993, James G. Arthur, 46, a lawyer from Arlington, Virginia, was sentenced to five years in federal prison for embezzling $2.4 million from eight elderly clients. Sonia Grenadier, a blind, 86-year-old grandmother, lost more than $100,000 from a trust fund account handled by Arthur.

During January 1993, a Massachusetts lawyer pleaded guilty to stealing $190,000 from an 84-year-old widow. The following month a jury in Wisconsin convicted a lawyer of stealing $110,000 from an 87-year-old woman. On Long Island, New York, another lawyer pleaded guilty to charges of defrauding investors, mostly elderly, out of $3 million.

Punch "Lawyers Swindling the Elderly" into the computer, press PRINT, and thousands of incidents roll to the floor: Lawyer Z. Herschel Smith stole $30,000 from a 98-year-old woman . . . Lawyer John P. Trevaskis Jr. was charged with stealing $233,000 from an elderly woman . . . Lawyer Perry Noble, administrator of a 90-year-old woman's estate, was temporarily suspended from practice pending an investigation into allegation that he misappropriated $143,000.

In scores of known cases lawyers have stolen money after requesting to handle tax returns for the elderly. Typically, the dishonest lawyer overstates what the older adult owes in state and federal taxes and then pockets the excess.

Sinking to new lows, at least 104 crooked lawyers have

written themselves into wills without the knowledge of their elderly clients; where there's a *will* there's a way.

At the reading of one will following the death of an 87-year-old woman, the executor read, "And to my loving lawyer I leave my house and $383,000. . . ."

"What!?" screamed the woman's 65-year-old daughter. "Mom hated that man!"

In that case the lawyer's scheme failed. Investigators found it very difficult to believe that the deceased woman had left so little to her loving children and so much to a lawyer she always complained about. The judge also learned that the same lawyer had surreptitiously entered his name into three other wills without the clients' knowledge.

One can't help but wonder, however, how many lawyers nationwide have actually been successful with this will scam.

As might be expected, crooked lawyers have also targeted the working class and the poor.

The *Philadelphia Inquirer* reported that on July 28, 1995, disbarred Pennsylvania lawyer David M. Weinfeld, 40, who admitted stealing millions of dollars from his working-class clients, was forced to face his victims.

During an eight-hour bankruptcy hearing in a windowless room, the personal injury lawyer admitted to theft after theft from his former clients.

Weinfeld, who mostly represented laborers who had become ill as a result of overexposure to asbestos, negotiated huge group settlements with insurers and asbestos manufacturers and then simply kept the money for himself.

One settlement for $706,000 was supposed to go to 220 of Weinfeld's clients. Weinfeld admitted he pocketed the money. Another settlement for $142,000 was supposed to be awarded to 44 clients. Weinfeld admitted he kept the money.

A third settlement for $2.5 million was supposed to go to 681 clients. Weinfeld admitted he stole the entire check.

Money that hundreds of working-class citizens were counting on to pay medical expenses, rent, and college tuition for their children was spent by one dishonest lawyer who purchased a lavish home and an office building, paid off personal debts, and enjoyed gourmet meals.

To help protect himself from hordes of angry clients, Weinfeld simply declared bankruptcy.

If the 747,000 honest lawyers in the United States ever hope to stop the jokes and dispel the rapidly growing shyster image of attorneys, they will have to get a lot tougher with and a lot less tolerant of their 153,000 crooked partners. It is time to get back to the *practice* of law instead of the *business* of law.

Stealing Insurance Money

Using a wide range of illegal schemes, more than 5000 lawyers during the past decade have pilfered money from insurance companies or pocketed insurance money belonging to their clients.

Some dishonest lawyers advise their clients to settle claims for one amount but actually negotiate a much larger settlement with the insurance company.

In one such case a lawyer advised a woman who was severely injured by a drunken driver to settle with the insurance company for $78,000. The lawyer, however, had already negotiated a $278,000 settlement with the drunken driver's insurance company. After cashing the check, the lawyer pocketed $200,000, kept $26,000 of the remaining $78,000 as his lawyer's fee and gave the injured woman $52,000.

Years later, investigators notified the injured woman

and two dozen other clients that the lawyer had pilfered huge portions of their insurance claims, but none of the victims received financial compensation from him.

Scores of dishonest lawyers have pocketed insurance checks awarded in personal-injury and medical malpractice cases and then told their clients that their settlements were still pending.

Elliot Stein, a lawyer in New York City, was charged with pocketing the $285,000 settlement of a lawsuit brought for a woman who suffered brain damage in an automobile accident. The indictment charged that Stein collected and cashed the check. But six years after the accident, Stein was still telling his client that the claim was "still pending."

Incredibly, at least 24 former clients of Stein's shouted similar complaints against him and filed claims totaling $609,000 with the Lawyers Fund for Client Protection, a state fund that reimburses people who say they have been cheated by their lawyers.

Although hundreds of people each year are still cheated out of insurance claims by their lawyers, new regulations that require insurance companies to notify clients when settlement checks are mailed to their lawyers has helped to curb the practice.

"The policy of writing the settlement check to the recipient, rather than the lawyer, has also helped to deter dishonest lawyers," said an insurance executor in Bethesda, Maryland. "But then we still see many cases in which the lawyer forges the recipient's signature."

Pennsylvania lawyer Ken Gross, 40, was informed in 1994 that he could no longer practice law after he pleaded guilty to defrauding a client of $57,000. Representing a client who had been hurt in a fall at a Kmart store, Gross settled the claim for $57,000. But the client never agreed to a settlement and did not know one had been reached. Gross forged the client's signature on the check and kept the money for himself.

The sad reality is that hundreds of lawyers have used forgery as a tactic and many have victimized dozens of clients.

Staged Accidents and Exaggerated Injuries

Two of the most popular insurance-fraud tactics, reaping billions of dollars for dishonest lawyers, are staged accidents and exaggerated injuries in real accidents. These tactics usually involve bribed witnesses, falsified evidence, scripted lies, and fraudulent reports from doctors and other professionals.

In a trial that symbolized the worst excesses of personal-injury law, New York lawyer Morris J. Eisen, 58, and six associates were convicted of bribing witnesses, manufacturing evidence, and stealing millions of dollars from insurance companies and taxpayers.

During the four-month, widely publicized trial, prosecutors proved that in 18 personal-injury cases the corrupt lawyers had bribed court personnel, paid people to testify as eyewitnesses, and fabricated evidence.

In one case the lawyers smashed a tire rim with a sledgehammer to exaggerate damage in an automobile accident, and in another case their investigators used a pickax to enlarge a pothole they claimed had caused an accident. One bribed witness who took an oath and testified in an accident case was actually in prison hundreds of miles away when the accident occurred. Coincidentally, the same convict just happened to be a witness at two separate accidents handled by Eisen's firm.

Since most of Eisen's phony lawsuits were against the city, it was the taxpayers who were making him rich. Eisen was found guilty of operating a 40-member law firm as a racketeering enterprise.

Staged and exaggerated personal-injury operations provide full-time work for many law firms.

On May 18, 1994, in Houston, Texas, a federal grand jury indicted attorney Harvey Holiman, 48, and charged that he was hired by a group of Bangladesh nationals for the sole purpose of processing fraudulent insurance claims. The indictment said that the group recruited individuals to stage whiplash injury accidents and cheated taxpayers out of more than $3 million.

In Philadelphia, Pennsylvania, on July 15, 1994, lawyer A. Terry Daly, 47, was charged with running an insurance ring that reaped at least $1.5 million in illegal profits. Daly solicited clients injured in fights and accidents and then falsified the cases to collect hefty insurance payoffs. Among other tactics, Daly rewrote doctors' reports to state that there were permanent disabling injuries when none existed, told a client to increase his automobile insurance for an upcoming staged accident, and scripted lies for his clients.

Most staged and exaggerated injury cases depend on "capping" operations to keep the scheme going. Capping involves runners who recruit people to participate in staged accidents.

A huge capping operation that bilked auto insurers out of more than $10 million was uncovered in Los Angeles during 1993. In that case, Warren Finn, a 55-year-old lawyer, pleaded guilty to charges that he participated in 1000 staged accidents and inflated claims cases.

"But to make the big money," said a disbarred lawyer who was caught staging accidents in the Midwest, "you need to be in cahoots with other professionals."

"It's just amazing how many of these fraud rings involve a whole circle of crooks including lawyers, doctors, and even police officers," explained a former chief investigator for a national insurance company. "I probably investigated a hundred such rings in my career . . . but knowing they are guilty and proving it in court are often two different things."

On March 13, 1995, Philadelphia lawyer Thomas S. Conroy pleaded guilty to being the ringleader of an elaborate slip-and-fall ring in which three doctors, a physical therapist, a chiropractor, and others fabricated personal-injury claims, medical bills, and other documents in order to bilk insurance companies out of $7 million.

Conroy had his scam down to a science. He collected photographs of potholes and other defects in pavements, parking lots, and sidewalks and, to make his scenarios more realistic, kept a weather log showing which days it had rained. He also hired runners who found others willing to file claims for bogus accidents.

Fortunately for the taxpayers, one of the people recruited by Conroy's fraud ring was an undercover FBI agent. The FBI agent testified in court that a lawyer working with Conroy pointed out a crack in the sidewalk and told him they could obtain $17,000 if he would trip on the crack and fake injuries. The undercover agent spent the next eight months going to doctors and physical therapists who fabricated and signed the necessary documents.

As a breed, dishonest lawyers have proven to be both conniving and creative when ripping off insurance companies and clients.

Fraudulent and Unethical Billing Practices

A 40-year-old lawyer appeared at the gates of heaven and loudly protested the injustice of being called at such a young age. "What do you mean you're only forty years old?" St. Peter replied. "According to the hours you've billed, we thought you were ninety-eight."

As a powerful multinational corporation with thousands of employees, the Chicago-based company was used to paying millions of dollars annually in legal fees. "Bills from law firms came in all the time and we just automatically wrote checks and sent them out," said a financial analyst for the company. "I guess they figured if you can't trust a lawyer who can you trust," he said with a laugh.

"But when low profits caused us to downsize and start laying people off, each division was asked to submit suggestions for reducing costs by 25 percent," the analyst explained. "As you might imagine, a lot of people had egg on their faces when an audit discovered that we had been overbilled $2,221,000 by several different lawyers."

Complaining that the fraudulent legal fees were swept under the carpet, the analyst, who had earned two master's degrees, surmised that the company executives "were more concerned about hiding their management mistakes from the shareholders than in recouping the lost money."

"In one case," said the analyst, "a lone lawyer handling a product-liability case charged us $151,200 for twenty-one days' work . . . and we paid it without blinking."

Explaining that the lawyer's rate was an "outrageous" $300 per hour, the analyst shouted, "He must have been Superman! To accrue a $151,200 bill the poor man would have had to have worked twenty-four hours per day for twenty-one days straight!"

Fraudulent and unethical billing practices by lawyers take many different forms and cost society over $2.5 billion annually.

During a flight from Washington, D.C., to California in early 1995, the author sat next to a lawyer in the first-class section of the aircraft. The lawyer, a specialist in international business law, was going to Los Angeles to visit seven corporate clients.

"Someone from my firm stops in every four months to sort of show the flag," he explained. "We like to press the flesh and let them know we're on top of things . . . sort of a public relations visit."

After exchanging some small talk about where we both lived and what high schools we both had attended in Maryland, the 47-year-old lawyer made some startling offhand comments about his billing practices.

"I'm only in L.A. for two days, so we make a lot more money on the airline tickets and hotel room than on my billable hours," he said.

When asked how a law firm could make money on the airline tickets and hotel room, the lawyer explained that each of the seven clients would be billed for his entire first-class airline ticket, hotel, and other expenses.

"Is that legal?" he was asked.

"Oh yeah, it's all on the up-and-up," he replied confidently. "Our agreement with each client states that they will pay for my travel expenses."

"Wouldn't it be more ethical if the seven clients were each charged for one-seventh of your expenses?" a third passenger asked.

"Probably," the lawyer responded with a wink and a smile, "but we'd sure lose a lot of money."

Jim Schratz, an auditor who works full-time investigating lawyers' bills, told *U.S. News & World Report* that he finds overcharges of 25 to 50 percent in 90 percent of the cases he is hired to examine.

Another auditor, who examined the legal fees a trucking firm paid during a two-year period, found that one lawyer had billed the business for 30 hours on a single day on 21 separate occasions. "How could they have missed that?" he asked rhetorically.

In Baltimore, Maryland, Edward S. Digges Jr., an internationally known product-liability lawyer, was sentenced to two and one-half years in prison, fined $30,000, and ordered to pay $1 million in restitution when he was caught overbilling Dresser Industries.

Dresser Industries, a Dallas-based manufacturing conglomerate, conducted an audit and discovered that Digges had charged $66,000 for medical research that had cost his law firm less than $400 and had billed the company at professional rates for work done by the firm's clerical employees. "The deeper the auditor dug the more dirt they discovered on Digges," said one investigator.

Digges, who represented the company in many asbestos-related lawsuits, used his ill-gotten gains to buy and refurbish a 310-acre country estate on the Eastern Shore of Maryland.

Dresser eventually won a $3.1 million legal malpractice award against Digges.

When Fredric N. Tulsky, a reporter for the *Philadelphia Inquirer*, investigated fees paid to court-appointed defense attorneys, he found that some lawyers were getting rich defending the poor.

Lawyer William J. Perrone charged Philadelphia $358,000 during a three-year period to represent the city's indigent criminals. The $358,000, which was not Perrone's only source of income, was at least seven times the average amounts paid to other attorneys during the same period of time.

Tulsky discovered that Perrone billed the city for 20 hours or more on 39 different days. On 18 separate occasions he billed for 24 or more hours in a day. And in three instances, Perrone reportedly billed the taxpayers for working more than 30 hours in a single day.

An affidavit that followed the investigative report charged that Perrone billed the city for cases that did not exist, charged the city for court hearings that never took place, and charged over and over again for doing the same research work.

Divorce lawyers, who are notorious for overbilling, have also been sharply criticized in recent years for purposely extending their cases (so they could continue to bill for hours) and for exploiting clients who are in an emotionally wrenching time in their lives.

In thousands of recorded cases, covering all 50 states, divorce lawyers have been accused of pressuring clients into giving up their homes and their assets to pay for blatantly extravagant legal fees.

Responding to public anger, many states now insist that clients be given a written fee schedule and itemized bills and forbid lawyers from taking a client's home for unpaid fees.

"If you're talking about fraudulent billing, the real crime is the extravagant fees these lawyers get for very little work," said a 50-year-old woman who received "peanuts" while her lawyer became a "multimillionaire" representing her and others in a class-action lawsuit.

The woman's complaint is shared by millions of other citizens who have participated in a variety of class-action lawsuits in recent years. When 4.2 million angry passengers gathered years-old flight receipts and filed a price-fixing lawsuit against the nation's major airlines, 37 law firms raced to file antitrust suits on behalf of air travelers.

Looking after their own interests rather than the interests of the plaintiffs, the lawyers agreed to an airline settlement in which passengers were offered discount coupons on airfares.

But passengers soon discovered that the terms of the settlement made the coupons practically worthless. Although the coupons had a total face value of $438 million, they could be redeemed for only a few dollars at a time.

One woman who flies weekly between Washington, D.C., and Long Island on fares of less than $200 complained that her coupons, valued at $25, could be used only if she purchased a ticket worth at least $250.

"These coupons will be worth about twenty dollars to me over a period of eighteen months," said another passenger, who had spent nine hours gathering the paperwork for the case. "My time on the case was worth one hundred eighty dollars."

Although the passengers were clearly the losers in this case, there were two big winners: the lawyers and the airlines. The lawyers who represented the passengers were awarded $16,012,500 in fees. And since the coupons do offer sufficient incentive that some consumers want to use them, the coupon settlement turned out to be a marketing bonanza for the airlines.

"If some people think they are getting a deal," said one airline employee, "they will take flights they normally wouldn't have taken just to save ten dollars."

Corporate defendants in class-action lawsuits are increasingly working out settlements in which consumers walk away with worthless scrip while their lawyers walk away with millions.

In 1994 some oat-based cereals like Cheerios were found to be tainted with pesticides. After heated legal negotiations, the consumers were each awarded a coupon for a free box of cereal, the lawyers walked away with $1.7 million, and General Mills stood to benefit from a slick marketing scheme.

"I had fists full of cereal coupons long before the lawyers got involved," said a woman who claims to have gotten ill from pesticides in food.

Without question, the majority of the class-action cases in recent years have been instigated by lawyers not to benefit the class, but to generate huge legal fees.

Another fee issue that gets people furious is the huge sums paid to bankruptcy lawyers while the creditors—the victims of the bankruptcy—don't see a dime.

On February 23, 1995, Oren Benton, the Denver uranium trader and 23 percent owner of the Colorado Rockies baseball team, filed for bankruptcy protection with $600 million in debts. If Benton's battered employees and creditors see any money at all, it will probably take years. The bankruptcy lawyers, however, billed the estate for more than $1 million.

Protecting Yourself from Overbilling

Auditors throughout the United States are reporting that lawyers are increasingly exaggerating their hours and charging for unnecessary work. Someone who is aware of how these tactics work and knows what questions to ask is less likely to be victimized.

Do not accept a broad-brush "for services rendered" type of bill; demand an itemized, easy-to-interpret accounting with breakdowns of hourly charges. Do not hesitate to challenge bills if you think you are being cheated.

Lawyers usually bill by the hour and charge from about $85 to about $400 an hour. Make sure you are not being billed at a lawyer's rate for work that was performed by a secretary. Insist that only lawyers and paralegals bill by the hour, and inquire about the professional status of everyone listed on the invoice. Make sure your expensive Harvard- or Yale-trained lawyer isn't charging at his rate for six hours of photocopying.

Lawyers typically keep track of their work in 10-minute increments; beware of the lawyer who never records segments less than a half hour. Did it take a half hour to write a three-sentence memo? Did it take a half hour for every telephone call?

Are you being charged to train less-experienced lawyers or to reeducate senior staff? If a new lawyer replaces the lawyer you've been paying for several months, the new lawyer will be spending a lot of time being "brought up to speed" on your case. The client should question the fairness of being billed to educate replacement lawyers. One law firm submitted a $250,000 bill for "educational conferences."

Are you being charged for extravagant meals and entertainment expenses that have nothing to do with your case? "Whenever we go to lunch," explained a female lawyer in Washington, D.C., "we draw straws to see whose client will be charged." Auditors warn that office parties and romantic meals with spouses and lovers are frequently squeezed into invoices.

If you are paying the travel expenses, ask your lawyer if he or she is also being reimbursed by other clients for the same airline and hotel fees. A lawyer traveling from Washington, D.C., to California made a $17,000 profit on each trip because seven different clients reimbursed him for the same travel expenses. In that case, each client should have been charged one-seventh of the travel expenses.

Are you being charged for "HVAC" (i.e., heating, ventilation, and air conditioning)? Many firms will try to get the client to pay for a pro rata share of the overhead. The smart client remembers the expression "whatever the traffic will bear" and balks at such charges.

Be alert to minimeetings that are recorded as "internal conferences." It's very easy for five lawyers to compare notes on your case for 25 minutes and then claim they were in conference for four hours. Sometimes auditors discover attorneys recording a few hours spent at a "conference" on a given day with no corresponding entry from the other lawyers allegedly in attendance. Sometimes one lawyer records the meeting as one hour while a second attendee records the same meeting as four hours.

Learn to read between the lines of vague language. When the invoice says "attention to" make sure it was *undivided* attention. Many lawyers bill for time paying "attention to" your case while they are in the rest room, driving home, or playing golf. Also be alert to blanket terms referring to travel. A $130 charge for "ground transportation" might be for a new pair of shoes; a $50 charge for "baggage handling" might be for a caddie. Is a $300-an-hour lawyer charging you to "set up and prepare a closing room"?

Are you being billed for the time it took the lawyer to bill you? Are you going to be billed for the time it takes to explain why you were billed for the time spent billing? Only if you allow it to happen.

When reviewing your invoice, don't forget the obvious: Check the math. Fed up with inflated billing schemes, more and more clients are requesting a flat rate or looking for firms that will work on a contingency fee.

Lawyers Stealing from Lawyers

On June 28, 1995, lawyer Webster L. Hubbell, a trusted, longtime friend of President Bill Clinton and a former law partner of Hillary Rodham Clinton, was sentenced to 21 months in prison for mail fraud and tax evasion and for stealing at least $394,000 from clients and his own law partners at the Rose Law Firm in Little Rock, Arkansas.

With his head bowed, the ashen-faced former high-ranking Justice Department official choked back tears and confessed that he had submitted false bills, phony expenses, and inflated fees on more than 400 occasions.

Hubbell's confession confirmed that a crook had been serving in one of the nation's top law-enforcement positions. It proved that Hubbell had been patting his law partners on the back with one hand while picking their pockets with the other.

Prosecutor W. Hickman Ewing Jr. showed how Hubbell had systematically looted his own law firm by simply filling out expense vouchers and using the money to pay off personal charges he had incurred on four MasterCards, three Visa cards, and three American Express cards.

When Hubbell stole from his partners he dishonored himself, disgraced his profession, and damaged the reputation of his firm. By stabbing his own partners in the back he committed the unkindest cut of all and joined an ever-growing fraternity of lawyers who genuinely believe they are above the law.

In Chicago, on December 26, 1994, federal authorities charged Gary L. Fairchild, 51, with stealing $236,000 from five clients, whom he fraudulently billed, and a whopping $548,218 from the prestigious law firm of Winston & Strawn, where he was the managing partner.

Earning more money than 97 percent of all U.S. citizens, Fairchild lived a lavish and enviable lifestyle. But despite reporting a joint 1992 income of $829,200 with his wife, who is also a lawyer, Fairchild was not satisfied. He found it necessary to rip off the taxpayers and the U.S. government by failing to report $204,000 of his income to the IRS. Arrogantly perceiving his clients as a means to an end, he rationalized that it was okay to put their hard-earned money in his pockets. And viewing loyalty, ethics, and honesty as terms used by suckers, he stole from his own partners, endangering their professional and financial futures.

Once he was caught red-handed, Fairchild admitted that by falsifying expense vouchers he was able to get the firm and his clients to pay for his children's dental bills, family air travel, hotels, health clubs, furniture for his home, catering fees, home improvements, plumbing expenses, Chicago Bulls play-off tickets, jewelry, and clothing. Unbeknownst to his partners, Fairchild also charged Winston & Strawn $8000 in rent for one of his apartments as well as $16,000 for a personal investment and fraudulently used firm money to pay off personal bank loans and to make a $50,000 payment on his income-tax return.

No novice to criminal deception, Fairchild used a wide range of tactics to steal money from his partners. Like many lawyers who steal from their own firms, Fairchild charged personal expenses on the firm's corporate credit cards and then submitted only the top portions of the bills, without the specific items listed, as business expenses. ("Maybe that's what Hubbell did when he charged those items from Victoria's Secret," chuckled an investigator familiar with the Fairchild and Hubbell cases.)

The *Chicago Tribune* reported that Fairchild also opened a fictitious client account, charged personal expenses to it, and then cleverly had the account written off as uncollectible at the firm's expense.

Although it is impossible to say exactly how many lawyers are stealing from their own firms—most dishonest lawyers are not caught and many of those caught are not prosecuted or publicized—a small sampling of the known cases revealed 62 lawyers who had stolen a total of $6,401,500 from their partners. With amounts stolen ranging from $9000 to over $1 million, the average amount each lawyer stole from his own firm, in this small sampling, was $103,250.

There are numerous cases in every state in which lawyers have embezzled money from their own partners.

On February 21, 1995, in Pennsylvania, police arrested John H. Wollman, a prominent lawyer, and charged him with stealing $295,036 from the firm of Lamb, Windle & McErlane, one of the largest and most influential law firms in Chester County. The affidavits say that Wollman endorsed 84 checks from clients and deposited them in his personal checking account rather than into the firm's coffers.

In North Carolina, lawyer Jim Blackburn pleaded guilty to embezzling $234,054 from his Raleigh law firm, faking a lawsuit for a client, and preparing 17 phony court orders by forging the signatures of judges. Blackburn, a former federal prosecutor, had helped convict former Army doctor Jeffrey MacDonald of the famous *Fatal Vision* murders.

And fugitive West Virginia lawyer Gordon Ikner, 48, was arrested in 1994 in a Texas motel room and charged with embezzling more than $250,000 from his law firm and clients.

Of course it is not only lawyers who are embezzling funds from law firms; in hundreds of cases secretaries, accountants, and paralegals have stolen large sums of money.

In 1993, a longtime secretary was charged with stealing $117,500 from the law firm of Duane, Morris & Heckscher in Philadelphia. Gail Montgomery, 50, was accused of stealing a $100,000 U.S. Treasury note and a client's check to the firm for $17,500.

On July 8, 1994, accountant Marion Jean Barrett, 51, was sentenced to two and one-half years in prison for embezzling $129,000 from her longtime client Erwin Alpern, a lawyer in Washington, D.C. Authorities believe that Barrett, who faked her own death and started a new life in Kentucky before being caught, actually stole "much, much more than $129,000."

Perusing a scroll-like printout of the "Lawyers Stealing from Lawyers" incidents, a Harvard lawyer in her mid-30s stood up from her leather chair, pointed to an empty office, and explained, "I never understood all those offensive lawyer jokes until an associate who used to be in that office stole $8000 of my earnings.

"But now I'm beginning to understand . . . the profession really is becoming a joke."

Fight Back with Humor

Sharing lawyer jokes is an excellent way to vent anger and an effective method of communicating displeasure—comic relief is an antidote to frustration. The closer a joke is to the truth the funnier it will be. People will stop making fun of lawyers when lawyers stop making a mockery of the law. A few of the author's favorite wisecracks are listed here to start the ball rolling:

> What's the difference between a lawyer and a vulture? The vulture doesn't get frequent-flyer miles.

> The attorney general has determined that your lawyer may be hazardous to your wealth.

> Why don't sharks eat lawyers? Professional courtesy.

> What's the difference between a lawyer and a catfish? One is an ugly, scum-sucking, bottom-feeding scavenger, and the other is a fish.

> Why do they bury lawyers 30 feet down? Because deep down lawyers are really good people.

> Terrorists hijacked an airliner full of lawyers on their way to a convention. They threatened that unless their demands were met, they would begin releasing one lawyer every hour.

Why did the post office have to recall its lawyer stamp? People didn't know which side to spit on.

Why does Washington have all the lawyers and New Jersey have all the toxic-waste dumps? New Jersey got first pick.

Bogus Lawyers

It happened to Shaw, Pittman, Potts and Trowbridge, the fifth-largest law firm in Washington, D.C. It happened to the Chicago law firm of Sonnenschein, Nath and Rosenthal. And it happened to Ferg, Barron and Gillespie and to Cofsky and Zeidman, two separate law firms in New Jersey.

During the past decade these law firms and scores of other law firms, companies, and organizations have been deceived into hiring bogus lawyers.

The law firm in Washington, D.C., discovered in 1995 that they had hired a lawyer who had been disbarred a decade earlier for financial fraud and had falsely claimed to be a graduate of Georgetown University Law School. The Chicago law firm discovered that a well-liked young partner had practiced law and represented clients for years without having passed the Illinois bar exam or having graduated from the University of Michigan Law School, as he claimed. And the two New Jersey law firms were both conned into hiring the same woman who, after clerking for judges, earned a lawyer's salary and charged a lawyer's fees even though she was not licensed to practice law, had never passed a bar exam, and didn't have a law degree.

Some lawyer impostors, like Steven Welchons of Madison County, New York, who never earned a college degree and never went to law school, have managed to fool their spouses, bosses, judges, and thousands of clients.

Welchons began his bogus law career in 1985 as an intern in the Oneida County public defender's office, where he impressed lawyer David Gruenewald.

The Associated Press reported that when Gruenewald moved to Watertown, New York, in 1988, to open a public defender's office, he hired Welchons without checking his claim that he was attending law school at Syracuse University.

Gruenewald then moved to Madison County in 1993 and again asked Welchons to join him. Apparently he never doubted Welchons' claim that he had finally graduated from Syracuse University and had passed the bar exam.

After representing nearly 2000 people in criminal court, Welchons' deception unraveled during June 1995 when a disgruntled client filed a complaint against him. Authorities following up on the complaint were unable to find his name listed on the registry of licensed attorneys.

Welchons' secret was suddenly out in the open, leaving his wife, his boss, his best friends, and 2000 clients wide-eyed with shock.

Experts predict that scores of Welchons' cases will have to be reprosecuted because they will be overturned on the grounds of inadequate representation.

Faced with charges that he impersonated a lawyer, falsely signed legal papers as a lawyer, and inadequately represented 2000 clients, Welchons attempted suicide by taking an overdose of nonprescription drugs.

As Welchons recuperated in the hospital room he learned something he would have known if he had attended law school: impersonating a lawyer is punishable by up to a year in jail, and falsely signing legal papers as a lawyer carries up to seven years.

From August 1987 to August 1995 authorities in the

United States investigated more than 275 individuals who falsely claimed to be lawyers.

There is no way of knowing how many fake lawyers are currently employed in the United States, but analysts believe that the number is certainly over 300. Many of these impostors, who were not disciplined or smart enough to earn a bachelor's degree, have proven to be slick enough to earn six-figure salaries as lawyers.

Different criminals impersonate lawyers for different reasons.

Frantz Maurice posed as an immigration lawyer in Miami and cheated hundreds of hopeful immigrants out of more than $122,000 and their dreams of a better life. The 37-year-old impostor was sentenced to four years in federal prison on April 22, 1994.

Serial murderer Johnny Meadows, who was convicted of raping and strangling seven women in and around Odessa, Texas, is believed to have posed as an attorney to lure women into a trap and to get money for legal work he was not qualified to conduct.

Some phony lawyers have practiced in the U.S. military and collected an officer's salary.

On September 1, 1994, in Quantico, Virginia, Captain Jeffrey Zander was found guilty of masquerading as a defense lawyer and wearing hero's decorations he had not earned.

The 39-year-old impostor, described by colleagues as a devoted family man and a well-respected officer, defended more than 50 clients on criminal charges at posts in Hawaii and Japan before authorities discovered he had fabricated his past and had never passed a bar exam.

Five years earlier, Zander had learned of a lawyer in California who shared his last name. Zander then created a bogus court order changing that person's name to his own and presented the document to the California State Bar Association, which issued him a membership card.

Zander also manufactured a fictitious DD214, the standard military discharge form, which falsely stated that he had earned a Bronze Star and a Purple Heart during the evacuation of Saigon while serving in the Navy from 1974 to 1975.

The Naval Investigative Service uncovered Zander's masquerade when they began investigating him for altering the official court record of a case he had handled.

A 38-year-old woman from Boise, Idaho, who was swindled out of $88,200 by a phony lawyer, aptly summed up the impersonation phenomenon when she stated: "The only thing worse than being swindled by a dishonest lawyer is being swindled by a dishonest phony lawyer."

Protecting Yourself from Impostors

Nationwide, scores of law firms and thousands of citizens have been duped and defrauded by lawyer impersonators, including so-called lawyers who have never graduated from college and/or graduate school; individuals who have never passed the bar examination; and former lawyers who have been disbarred but continue to practice. Recognizing that phony diplomas, IDs, and résumés are about as common as lawsuits, the smart consumer will take several precautions before hiring a lawyer:

- Check with the state bar association or the agency that admits lawyers to practice to determine that the lawyer is licensed.

- Obtain a certified transcript directly from the law school for any newly hired lawyer.
- When you hire an experienced lawyer, obtain a certificate of good standing from the disciplinary agency in the jurisdiction where the applicant has practiced.
- Conduct a thorough, probing reference check and an in-depth personal interview. Ask lots of questions.

The Lawyers Fund for Client Protection

Though they differ widely from state to state, the Lawyers Fund for Client Protection has been established by the good lawyers to reimburse people who have been robbed by dishonest lawyers. In most cases the funds are financed by the licensing and registration fees that lawyers pay to the state.

Funds typically make payments to victims whose lawyers have been found guilty of embezzling or misusing client money. But there are two primary problems: Most states have a $50,000 to $100,000 cap on how much can be reimbursed (hundreds of victims each year lose much more than $100,000 to dishonest lawyers), and, with an ever-increasing number of victims, most funds run out of money before everyone can be reimbursed.

One lawyer gone amok might victimize 50 clients before he is caught, and a single state might have 100 lawyers embezzling money at the same time. Jack B. Solerwitz, a crooked New York lawyer, victimized 86 clients who then applied to the state fund for almost $3 million. Since the fund's assets were only $2 million, the activities of one unleashed lawyer put the fund in the hole.

The Lawyers Fund for Client Protection is an honorable step in the right direction; if there is to be confidence in the legal system, victims will have to be compensated and the good lawyers will have to get tough with the bad lawyers. But with fraud at an all-time high, the good lawyers will have to get a lot more aggressive or lobby for a lot more money.

Tips for Fighting Back

Here are some tips to save yourself the grief and embarrassment of being victimized by a dishonest lawyer.

- Conduct a thorough investigation and background check before hiring a new lawyer. Ask a lot of questions.

- Demand an itemized, easy-to-interpret bill with breakdowns of hourly charges. Do not hesitate to challenge a bill if you think you are being cheated.

- If you are paying travel expenses, ask whether your lawyer is also being reimbursed by other clients serviced on the same trip.

- Balk at charges for office overhead. Many firms will try to get the client to pay a pro rata share of the heating, ventilation, and air conditioning.

- Are you being charged for the time it took a lawyer to bill you? Are you going to be billed for the time it takes to explain why you were billed for the time spent billing? Only if you allow it to happen.

- When reviewing your invoice, check the math.

- Support ethics training for lawyers. Moving to counter growing dissatisfaction with the legal profession, a committee of New York State's leading judges and lawyers stressed the importance of such ethics training for law students as well as for new and experienced lawyers. The committee recommended establishing an ethics institute in New York modeled after the Texas Center for Legal Ethics and Professionalism.

- Publicize a lawyer's misdeeds. Although lawyers convicted of felonies should be fined and jailed like any other criminal, we also need to make better use of publicity as a deterrent.

- Watch out for lawyers who may show signs of substance abuse. The data clearly indicates that a high percentage of corrupt lawyers have an intimate relationship with drugs and alcohol.

Cheating Charities

The United Way Scandal

On June 22, 1995, William Aramony, 67, a disgraced former president of United Way of America, was sentenced to seven years in federal prison for defrauding the charity of more than $1 million to support a playboy lifestyle of young girlfriends, fancy restaurants, exotic travel, and lavish living.

After a lengthy, nationally publicized trial in Alexandria, Virginia, complete with lurid details of Aramony's sex life, thousands of United Way contributors were left shaking their heads in disgust and wondering if they had been suckers to donate money.

During the trial, three young sisters who grew up in a trailer park near Gainesville, Florida—Lisa, Lori, and Lu-Ann Villasor—told a wide-eyed jury about their travels and adventures with Aramony.

Lisa Villasor met Aramony in 1986 when she sat next to him on an airplane. Lisa was 22 years old at the time and

Aramony, the president of the nation's biggest charity, was 59 years old and married.

Attracted to Lisa from the start, Aramony arranged a job for her at United Way's Virginia headquarters. The two soon began a sexual relationship and traveled together, at United Way's expense, to San Francisco, New York, and other locations. Lisa testified that she ended the relationship within five months.

Meanwhile, Lori Villasor, who was then age 17, had come to live with her sister Lisa in her studio apartment in Alexandria. Lori also became romantically involved with Aramony and continued a relationship with him until July 1990.

The jury learned that Aramony kept Lori on as a paid mistress at the charity's expense and that the lovers junketed to Las Vegas, New York, and other cities together. For a Christmas present in 1989 the two used United Way money for a 12-day vacation in London and Egypt for which Aramony's travel agency noted that "cost is no object!" A $2330 bill for just one day in Egypt included a limousine, guides, champagne, flowers, and a cruise on the Nile.

Prosecutors noted that United Way contributors paid for at least 34 trips by Aramony to Gainesville, Florida, hometown of the three Villasor sisters, even though he conducted no business there. During frequent trips to New York, Lori and Aramony charged the charity $70,000 for chauffeurs alone. United Way contributors also purchased a facsimile machine for Lori so she could send love notes to Aramony.

"The money Aramony spent on roses for his young girlfriends could have fed three starving children for a year," noted an investigator close to the case.

Using charity coffers as his own personal war chest and United Way as his fiefdom, Aramony, the self-appointed dictator-king, also purchased and decorated a $383,000 condominium in New York City and diverted $325,000 to a Florida company he created and controlled.

LuAnn Villasor, the third sister to testify, also had some depressing news concerning how charitable dollars are being spent. She too had a relationship with the United Way president and fondly remembered the happy times that started with a trip to Las Vegas and New York in 1989, a high school graduation gift from Aramony.

As Aramony sat stoically in the courtroom, a parade of former lovers and female employees whom he had sexually harassed testified as to how he had used United Way's resources and his position as president to get his way sexually.

Of course there was an excuse for Aramony's criminal and unethical behavior. Aramony's lawyer actually argued that a mental condition had caused his brain to shrink.

"The real crime is that his salary was so huge," complained the vice president of an insurance company. "There are plenty of bright, energetic executives who could do better than Aramony for half the price." Aramony's salary was $390,000 a year plus generous bonuses, plus anything he could steal.

The Aramony/United Way of America scandal gave the public an inside peek at how some charitable organizations are mismanaged. And as James Bausch, president of the National Charities Information Bureau, told the *Washington Post*: "An age of naive innocence has been stripped away."

Frequency of Charity Fraud

Although there are no empirical studies on the frequency of fraudulent acts committed by charities (most embezzlers are never caught), existing data strongly suggests that a wide range of criminals are stealing more than $21 billion from charities in the United States each year.

An executive of one national charity rationalized that it was okay to use tax-deductible dollars to pay for his child's college tuition, lease an expensive car for his wife, and remodel his home. Another charity paid $187,000 for its executive director's wedding reception and listed the expense as "fund raising."

But this disgraceful theft of charitable contributions does not have to occur. The public's donations do not have to go into the pockets of greedy criminals. If the federal and state governments would wake up to the widespread problem of charity fraud, increase the number of trained auditors and investigators, and prosecute all offenders, the elimination of this $21-billion annual theft might allow an extra $1 million to be contributed to 21,000 deserving causes.

The $21 billion stolen from charities each year does not include the money that is lost through mismanagement and poor judgment. It does not include the money that is legally diverted from charities' stated missions (a high percentage of all charity revenues go for start-up, fund-raising, and administrative costs). And it does not include the billions of dollars in tax revenues lost because undeserving organizations have been awarded tax-exempt status.

Tax-Exempt Status

The public tax-exempt charity industry in the United States brings in more than $400 billion in revenues annually. The sources of this income include individual donations (Americans contributed about $130 billion to charities in 1995), government grants (i.e., taxpayers' money), investment income, and sideline commercial enterprises. Money earned from commercial enterprises is considered taxable income, but a high percentage goes untaxed because of fraud, creative bookkeeping, and poor oversight.

We are being too charitable to charities. An estimated 30 percent of the 500,000 charities in the United States do not deserve a tax-exempt status.

When most people think of tax-exempt nonprofit organizations, they usually think of Good Samaritan groups such as the American Red Cross or the Salvation Army, organizations that genuinely help the needy. But Congress also awards tax-exempt status to hundreds of big businesses, special-interest groups, and even lobbying organizations.

The PGA (Professional Golfers' Association of America) Tour, the Mutual of America Life Insurance Company, the Major League Baseball Players Association, and the Open Software Foundation all enjoy tax-exempt status even though they do not fulfill traditional charitable roles and, arguably, contribute little to the so-called public good. Adding to the taxpayers' ire is the reality that the top executives of the above-mentioned tax-exempt nonprofit organizations earn salaries of $4.1 million, $1.2 million, $932,000, and $1.4 million respectively.

Treating the tax-exempt status as a right, rather than a privilege, Congress has created a fire-breathing Charity Monster that is burning good-hearted Americans and taking crippling bites out of the nation's treasury. Despite all the disclosures and hearings on Capitol Hill—despite billions of dollars in tax revenues lost because of undeserved exemptions—the government continues to approve tax-exempt status for 24,000 new charities each year.

Biting the hand that feeds it, the Charity Monster is out of control.

Since charities do not contribute much revenue to the government, the Internal Revenue Service, the agency that regulates nonprofit organizations, audits less than 0.5 percent of all tax-exempt organizations. Even though thousands of charities are guilty of fraud and theft, the IRS revokes only about 35 licenses each year.

Lacking staff and resources, the IRS and other charity watchdogs are frequently fooled by phony "program services" statements, reports that downplay the amount of funding that is gobbled up by fund-raising and administrative expenses and exaggerate the amount of money spent on the stated purpose of the charity. Using creative bookkeeping techniques, many unscrupulous charities have been able to look good on paper while contributing nothing to the needy.

Fraudulent charities have been coddled too long, too much unchecked power has been given to smiling executives, and thousands of charities have been provided with a license to steal. It is time to scrutinize charities more closely, get tough with offenders, stop being fooled by scam "program services" reports and charming but dishonest chief executive officers, and start learning from past mistakes. The public needs to ask more questions, implement more checks and balances, demand reader-friendly accounting of charitable finances and disbursements, publicize fraudulent activities, communicate the tactics the crooks are using, and take advantage of one of the most effective weapons against fraud: awareness.

A Foundation of Fraud

The fall of the Pennsylvania-based Foundation for New Era Philanthropy clearly illustrates that there is a great deal of greed as well as generosity in the charity business.

On May 15, 1995, the Foundation for New Era Philanthropy, which had promised double-your-money windfalls to hundreds of nonprofit institutions and private investors, filed for bankruptcy, listing an incredible $551 million in liabilities and $80 million in assets.

Shock waves from New Era's unexpected collapse reverberated worldwide, threatening hard times and even extinction for many schools, museums, ministries, libraries, and other groups that had entrusted their futures to the foundation.

Amid allegations of fraud and deceit, New Era's chief executive, John G. Bennett Jr., 57, is suspected of orchestrating the biggest charitable scam in history and is being investigated by the FBI, the IRS, the Securities and Exchange Commission, and a growing army of lawyers.

Investigators believe that New Era Philanthropy misappropriated at least $55 million during the first four months of 1995 alone, and that Bennett may have diverted much of the fortune to private businesses he controlled. "So that's why Bennett didn't need to draw a salary at New Era," said a private donor who stands to lose her entire $300,000 contribution. "I hear he also received huge consulting fees and employed his wife and daughter."

Like many other white-collar criminals before him, Bennett apparently operated a giant Ponzi or pyramid scheme in which money from new investors was used to pay off earlier investors. A Ponzi scheme requires an ever-growing group of investors to keep it afloat.

By constantly robbing Peter to pay Paul, Ponzi schemes are able to pay generous returns to some investors. Typically, these happy investors will tell their friends about their good fortune and the friends will also invest in the scheme.

But when these same investors continue to reinvest their money (usually in larger and larger amounts) they eventually lose everything when the scheme collapses.

New Era promised potential investors that they would double their money. All the investor had to do was deposit the money with New Era for six months and allow the foundation to keep the funds in its own brokerage account rather than in escrow.

New Era explained to donors that their money would be matched by anonymous, extremely wealthy philanthropists who didn't have the time to find worthy causes and were relying on New Era to do it for them. "It was a cock-and-bull story, and a lot of us fell for it," said the woman who contributed $300,000. "But it was simply too good to be true."

When Bennett's world came crashing down on May 15, 1995, he admitted to his staff that the anonymous, extremely wealthy donors didn't exist.

In addition to almost 200 nonprofit organizations that participated in New Era's program, about 150 wealthy individuals were also tempted by the foundation's double-your-money promise. Former Treasury Secretary William E. Simon gave $6.5 million to New Era; Laurance S. Rockefeller gave $11.3 million; and John C. Whitehead, former cochairman of Goldman, Sachs & Co., gave nearly $1 million.

Tax investigators are now trying to learn if some New Era donors illegally doubled their taxable deductions, even though they were entitled to deduct only the amount they actually gave to New Era.

New Era's 1993 IRS tax return claims that the foundation donated $34 million in charitable gifts that year. The only problem is that many of the alleged recipients of these charitable contributions report that they never saw a penny and never even heard of the Foundation for New Era Philanthropy.

Millions of good and trusting citizens worldwide who genuinely want to do some good in this world contributed hard-earned dollars to hundreds of charities of their choice: a home for retarded children, an endowment for missionaries in China, a scholarship for a talented inner-city musician. Believing that they would get something for nothing, the leaders of these charities took the money given to them by their donors and gave it to Bennett and his get-rich-quick foundation.

The bottom line is that hundreds of millions of charitable dollars—dollars that could have been used to find cures for diseases or feed hungry children—have disappeared into greedy pockets.

New Era went bankrupt owing huge sums of money to 300 universities, churches, and other uninsured creditors. Lancaster Bible College is owed $16.9 million, and the Young Life International Service Center in Colorado Springs is owed $11 million. The Christian Broadcasting Network lost $100,000; the First Baptist Church in Glenside, Pennsylvania, lost $77,200; and the Academy of Natural Sciences may have lost as much as $2.7 million.

Even the United Way, the giant, scandal-plagued national charity, placed $2 million of their donors' money with New Era in hopes of getting $4 million back.

With 300 complaints filed, the New Era investigation will likely continue for years. But regardless of the findings, regardless of any prison sentences that might be handed out, the final result of New Era's double-your-money scheme is that hundreds of charities have been deprived of money that generous donors contributed on their behalf.

Bingo and Casino Nights

When police arrested Kenny Graham in 1985 he was charged and convicted of conspiring to procure females for prostitution. That's a fancy way of saying he was convicted for being a pimp. Then in 1994, at age 50, Graham was arrested and fingerprinted in Henrico County, Virginia, this time charged with stealing more than $700,000 in cash proceeds from his charitable bingo business.

Charitable bingo is big business in the United States, bringing in nearly $4 billion in cash annually. Permeated with fraud, misrepresentation, diversion of funds, and racketeering, it is also a business that frequently cheats the charities it claims to sponsor. It is a business in which hundreds of Kenny Grahams are getting rich.

Since bingo is considered gambling in Virginia, Michigan, Florida, and most other states, it is usually allowed only if all proceeds, minus actual business expenses, go to charity. In most cases the name of the charity receiving the proceeds must be posted in the bingo hall and only unpaid charity members are allowed to run the games. But rules and reality are often two different things; white-collar crooks are masters at skirting, bending, and breaking the laws.

There are many ways a dishonest bingo entrepreneur can pocket charitable contributions, but the schemes usually involve rigged games, inflated rental rates for bingo parlors, phantom employees, and kickbacks from vendors who supply transportation, security, janitorial services, and so forth.

In step one of the typical bingo rip-off, a for-profit bingo hall company will rent a modest hall and furnish it with long rows of inexpensive tables. The management company then recruits charities to rent the hall at exorbitant rates.

One company that "skimmed millions of dollars" purportedly destined for needy children rented a large, deserted warehouse for $4500 per month or $150 per day. At that rate, the company was paying only $75 for each of the two daily bingo sessions.

But the management company, run by two ex-convicts, charged the charity $450 per day or $13,500 per month, which was three times what the management company was paying. Interestingly, at $13,500 per month the charity was paying $162,000 per year in rent for a dilapidated warehouse that had an assessed value of only $191,000.

The management company also charged the charity three times the going rate for transportation, security guards, janitorial services, utilities, and supplies.

Since exorbitant rates were charged for rent and services, the management company was able to deduct inflated business expenses and increase its cut of the charitable proceeds.

What does this all mean in terms of profits for the management company and the charity? Although an average of 127 bingo players spent approximately $2921 each day on bingo games, the owners showed a much lower rate of income because they deducted the *inflated* business expenses. The management company paid a maximum of $525 per day in rent and expenses but charged the charity (a deducted business expense) an inflated $2870 for rent, services, and several phantom employees.

This means that the two co-owners of the management company (whose prison monikers were reportedly "Knuckles" and "Fat Man") made a profit of $2396 per day or $874,540 per year for this one bingo parlor. "Bingo!" the con artists probably screamed as they counted their cash.

On paper the needy children made $51 per day—one dollar more than the $50 minimum stipulated in the management contract—or $18,615 per year.

But the con game was not over. What happens when the management company and the charity are either in cahoots or are one and the same?

In this operation, "Knuckles" and "Fat Man" were "almost certainly" in cahoots with a dishonest charity director who not only paid kickbacks to the two ex-convicts but claimed that "operating and start-up costs ate up most of the charitable contributions."

So how much of the $18,615 per year did the children actually receive? Practically nothing.

Dishonest operators also rip off charities by rigging the bingo games and sharing the winnings with an accomplice.

Indictments charging "misapplication of funds" usually involve two types of bingo contests. In the more frequent scam, a player will shout "Bingo!" and claim to have a winning card in a $1000 or $2000 game. A corrupt bingo employee then falsely verifies the player's card as a winner, and later splits the prize money with the player.

The other rip-off involves variations of the high-dollar "Do It" game where a player picks some numbers, writes them on a card, and drops the card into a locked box before the winning numbers are selected.

In scores of proven cases and probably thousands of unproven cases, players in on the scam waited until the numbers were called and then wrote them down and secretly slipped the card into the box, guaranteeing wins of $10,000 to $100,000.

Las Vegas-style "casino nights" have also proven to be extremely lucrative for con artists.

Acting on a tip from a woman who did not appreciate being deceived, police in Prince George's County, Maryland, raided a casino night fund-raiser held at a local fire station and charged Norman A. Smith with stealing more than $400,000.

Smith had been renting the space for nine months and held a Las Vegas-style fund-raiser twice a week allegedly to collect money for the Ardmore Developmental Center for the physically and mentally challenged.

As is so often the case, one inquisitive participant caused the downfall of a corrupt entrepreneur. After playing roulette and blackjack at the fund-raiser, a female participant returned home and discovered, to her dismay, that she had left her eyeglasses at the fire station.

When the woman called directory assistance for the Ardmore listing, she was given two telephone numbers. One number was for a business in Largo, Maryland, that had been set up by Norman Smith. The second number was for the real charity, which was in another city.

Fortunately, the woman called the real charity and Ardmore officials informed her that they were not the sponsors of any casino night fund-raiser. The woman's second call was to the police.

Like so many other dishonest gaming operators, Smith had apparently submitted a fraudulent application to run a charitable fund-raiser and then proceeded to raise a huge amount of money for his favorite charity—himself.

Medical Charities

On October 30, 1995, police arrested Frank Williams, 54, director of the American Parkinson's Disease Association, and charged him with embezzling more than $870,000 from the charity.

Williams confessed in *Fortune* magazine that he had been stealing contributions for ten years, and stated: "I'd go home at night and say to myself, '. . . I'm embezzling $80,000 a year. What the hell am I doing?' " But like many other charity executives, Williams would go to work the next day and rationalize that he, not the patients, deserved the money.

While receiving a generous annual salary of $109,000, Williams supplemented his income by stealing more than $80,000 a year tax free from people suffering from Parkinson's disease.

The Association, which has an annual budget of about $5 million, hired a private investigative firm and alerted federal authorities when it suspected embezzlement. One investigator familiar with the case told the author, "It should have been easy to catch him ten years ago. They just trusted him too much and were blinded by his good-guy profile."

Medical charities, often considered the most sacred of all causes, are not exempt from white-collar crime.

During the past decade, billions of dollars have been stolen from more than 200 medical charities. In Illinois, a telemarketing firm reportedly collected $9 million for the National Children's Cancer Society but allegedly gave only $800,000 to the children. In Pennsylvania, Nancy Anne Stedman, 41, was convicted of embezzling $129,627 from the American Lung Association. And in Boston, Massachusetts, a federal judge ordered Dr. Bernardo Nadal-Ginard, a former Harvard Medical School professor, to repay nearly $6.5 million he "misappropriated" from the Boston Children's Heart Foundation.

In 644 other known cases, phony telemarketers and door-to-door con artists collected money for nonexistent patients who were allegedly suffering from burns, car accident injuries, and rare diseases. Generous, good-hearted citizens reached deep into their pockets and unwittingly subsidized criminals in all 50 states.

The reality is that thousands of men and women have stolen between $1000 and $1 million from medical charities. This problem is hurting us greatly.

Living Off AIDS

On July 7, 1992, Prem S. Sarin, 57, a former administrator at the National Institutes of Health in Bethesda, Maryland, and one of the nation's leading AIDS researchers, was convicted of pocketing $25,000 earmarked for AIDS research and falsifying financial disclosure statements.

In the fall of 1993, the executive director of a nonprofit AIDS foundation in the Southwest was arrested and charged with forging checks and stealing thousands of dollars from the charity. The foundation, which relies on private donations and government grants, provides rent, transportation, food, and other services to AIDS patients.

And during March 1995, in Miami, Florida, the FBI and federal prosecutors began investigating a nationally known AIDS expert for allegedly setting up a phantom laboratory to siphon off at least $250,000 in federal grant money donated for AIDS research.

While thousands of people are dying from AIDS each

year, thousands of con artists are lining their pockets and living the high life with AIDS dollars.

Looting charitable coffers in all 50 states, different criminals have discovered many different and devious ways to make a living off the AIDS epidemic. Some crooks collect donations and put the proceeds into their own pockets; some AIDS administrators have written checks to phantom consultants and counseling services; and some criminals have used blackmail and murder to steal from AIDS accounts.

Francis Stoffa, the affable former head of the Philadelphia AIDS Task Force, was accused of using a variety of different tactics to steal $200,000 from AIDS victims.

On March 22, 1995, a 36-count grand jury presentment accused Stoffa of writing 154 agency checks worth $84,000 to himself, of charging expensive Atlantic City vacations to the AIDS task force, and of using an agency American Express card to purchase clothing, a health club membership, and other personal items.

"While AIDS victims were living and dying in subways, Stoffa was apparently stuffing down steaks and squandering our fortunes at the roulette wheel," complained a 41-year-old HIV-positive heterosexual male. "He should be charged with murder, not embezzlement."

Diversifying his corruption like most people diversify investments, Stoffa reportedly submitted receipts for such items as floor decking, tools, and cedar lining that were purportedly for the agency food bank but were probably used for his own home improvements.

As director of the agency, Stoffa collected all private donations, signed agency checks, and invoiced all contracts with the government. He would personally collect money from fund-raising events and turn the money in, 24 to 48 hours later, counted and bundled. But several agency members complained that a lot more money had been raised than Stoffa reported.

Descending to the lowest rung of human behavior, a wide range of criminals are stealing millions of dollars each year from AIDS service agencies, AIDS charities, and AIDS patients. Like most white-collar offenders, these criminals are stealing much more than money; they are betraying trust, embezzling hope, and stealing lives.

"My hope is that contributors do not put everyone in the same category as Francis Stoffa," said an AIDS activist and mother of a 23-year-old man who died from the disease. "Education, research, and money are our best weapons against this horrible disease; we need to stop the criminals, not the giving."

Phony Police and Fire Department Charities

In 1988, police raided 15 sites in New York City and Long Island and brought down a bogus fund-raising ring that claimed to aid the families of police officers killed in the line of duty. During the 10 years the fraudulent charity had been in operation, the generous citizens of the United States had happily reached deep into their pockets and contributed $6 million to the fast-talking solicitors.

What thousands of Americans didn't realize is that they were actually contributing to the crooks, not the cops. Of the $6 million collected supposedly for charity, the con artists reportedly stuffed $5,960,000 into their own pockets and used a measly $40,000 to purchase insurance for a few police officers on Long Island.

"I still contribute," said a store owner after learning of

the scandal. "But now I won't be hoodwinked by telemarketers, and I usually just send a check directly to the family."

From June 1988 to June 1995 phony police and fire department charities in the United States cheated well-meaning citizens, police, and firefighters out of at least $110 million. Hundreds of these scams have been reported nationwide.

Fortunately, most states are beginning to view these schemes as unacceptable drains on the economy and are increasingly taking legal action.

On April 29, 1993, the state of Massachusetts filed suit against Samuel Farrell, charging that he raised $345,000 for a sham charity that deceived donors by falsely claiming that the group was made up of police officers and that the donations would be used to fight domestic violence and child abuse. The suit alleged that only $8000 of the $345,000 went to charity. On August 24, 1994, the state attorney general in New York filed a suit against Carlo Batchelor, charging that he fraudulently raised $143,000 by claiming to be collecting money for families of firefighters who died in the line of duty. And in Florida, on June 22, 1995, authorities arrested Darryl Richard Bruggemann, 33, a telemarketer, and charged him with fraudulently soliciting nearly $200,000 in charitable contributions on behalf of four police and Vietnam War veterans' groups. None of the police or veterans' groups were aware of the fund-raising effort.

One con artist in New York fraudulently raised tens of thousands of dollars by claiming that the money would be given to the families of firefighters James F. Young, Christopher J. Siedenburg, and John J. Drennan, who died in the line of duty.

Vina Drennan, the widow of Captain Drennan, who died May 7, 1994, after 50 days in a hospital burn unit, was naturally furious that a criminal would try to exploit her husband's painful death.

Quoted in the *New York Times*, Mrs. Drennan stated: "I suppose if this man could have watched for 15 minutes to see how my husband suffered, it would have made him understand that he should feel ashamed."

Charity Fraud International

The charity fraud problem, of course, is also international; every country in the world reports cases of theft from charities.

On May 25, 1995, in Nairobi, UNICEF's executive director, Carol Bellamy, reported that the United Nations Children's Fund lost $10 million to fraud and mismanagement from its Kenya office in 1993 and 1994 alone. The fraud included payments for nonexistent services, double billing, insurance claims for bogus medical problems, and payments to phantom contractors.

One of the most blatant and costly thefts from a charity by a single individual occurred in England. On March 27, 1992, Rosemary Aberdour, 30, director of a charity that raises money for London's National Hospital for Neurology and Neurosurgery, was sentenced to four years in prison for plundering $3.5 million in contributions on a fantasy lifestyle of jewels, cars, expensive travel, and lavish parties.

Aberdour pleaded guilty to 17 charges of deception and admitted she siphoned $3.5 million that was supposed to help patients suffering from Parkinson's and Alzheimer's diseases, multiple sclerosis, and epilepsy.

A master of deception, Aberdour pretended to be a Scottish earl's daughter and stole from the sick so that she could play with the rich. The bogus aristocrat, who was actually the daughter of a radiologist, used the embezzled money to rent a riverside London penthouse for $3450 a week and had a chauffeur-driven Bentley automobile. She spent $110,600 of the charity's money on her 29th birthday party and gave herself a pair of earrings that cost $62,190.

Rubbing shoulders with royalty, "Lady" Aberdour hired a helicopter to take her and a friend from London to Wales, where she splashed out $70,000 for a lunch at a Welsh castle. The lunch included heraldic trumpeters, a knight on a white charger, and a chauffeur-driven limousine for her pet Labrador retriever.

In 1990, Aberdour forged a charity check and wasted $207,000 in contributions on a Chinese ball at the Savoy Hotel. The classy hotel apparently wasn't up to snuff for the occasion, so Aberdour paid organizers to build waterfalls and special bridges across small rivers in the ballroom.

"Charity work is bloody fun," she must have thought.

Probably thinking the fantasy and the money would never end, Aberdour even planned a glamorous wedding in which she hired ships and a plane to ferry guests to and from various locations. The plans called for her to once again redecorate the Savoy Hotel for the reception, this time at a cost of $77,640.

A reception for royalty would not be complete without jewelry and flowers, so Aberdour forged additional checks on the charity's account and spent $293,300 on diamonds and rubies and $91,400 on flowers.

The good news is that the would-be princess is now a prisoner. The bad news—and it's always the same in these cases—is that the would-be recipients of the charity are not getting the help they need and are suffering a much greater sentence.

Tips for Fighting Back: Rules That Apply When Donating to *Any* Charity

- Please help society and the needy by contributing to charity. Identify a worthy cause, give something back to life, and do something good for the world. But be smart and be careful. A wide range of criminals, including corrupt charity administrators, steal more than $21 billion contributed to charities each year. In recent years thousands of phony charities have cropped up in the United States and thousands of employees of legitimate charities are known to have pocketed contributions. Don't help those who are only helping themselves. Don't help a crook get rich.

- Do not donate your hard-earned money until you have received information *in writing* about the charity. Always ask what percentage of your contribution actually goes to the needy as opposed to fund-raising costs. Watchdog groups say that a minimum of 65 percent should actually go to the stated cause. There are many cases in which millions of dollars were collected for a particular cause but not one penny actually went to the needy or the stated purpose. Instead, the money was spent on overhead (i.e., extravagant salaries and vacations for charity administrators, golf outings, fancy offices, mailings, and start-up expenses). Be aware that when charities hire outside professional fund-raisers the charities sometimes receive only 10 to 20 percent of what is collected and frequently end up losing money.

  In 1994 the National Trust for Historic Preservation hired a professional fund-raiser to collect donations in

Massachusetts. The group raised about $113,000, but none of the money found its way to the trust; all of the money and more ended up in the pocket of the fund-raiser. The fund-raiser billed the trust for more than $116,000 in management fees, leaving the trust owing $3383. People who believed they were helping an important cause were actually donating their money to a fund-raiser, who, it can be assumed, was very happy to receive the charitable contributions. Ironically, while the generous contributors thought they were giving $113,000 to the National Trust for Historic Preservation, the trust ended up $3383 poorer.

Unfortunately, there are hundreds of horror stories. After hiring a solicitor, Common Cause ended up $12,000 in the red. The expenses of the solicitor far exceeded the amount it raised. A solicitor for the National AIDS Brigade raised $410,000 but gave only $37,950 to the charity.

- Concerned contributors should request to review a group's charitable tax return, called an IRS 990, the most informative and official document available to donors. The IRS 990 gives detailed information concerning how a charity spent its contributions. Dividing expenses into three categories—programs, administration, and fund raising—the form lists the salaries and expense accounts (very important) of key executives, and the amounts the charity paid for fund-raisers, telephone bills, travel, legal fees, postage, conventions, and conferences. The law does not require a tax-exempt charity to send out a copy of its IRS 990 (although forthright charities do so for a small postage and handling fee), but it must make its three most recent 990s available for public inspection during normal business hours on the day of request. A charity that does not comply with such a request can be fined $5000 by the IRS. The charity is not required to give a copy of the tax return, only to let it be viewed. Charities are allowed to withhold, for privacy purposes, the names and addresses of donors.

- Before contributing money to charities many people are now asking, "What is the annual salary of the top executives?" If the salaries of the top executives are outrageously high, more and more people are refusing to contribute. "My money isn't going to the needy, it's lining some executive's pocket," complained a retired elementary-school teacher. Many directors of nonprofit charities make more than the President of the United States. William Aramony, the disgraced president of United Way of America, earned $390,000 a year plus generous bonuses.

- Don't make impulsive decisions. Before contributing, ask questions, take your time, refuse to be pressured. Don't be fooled simply because the cause seems official and the organizers "seem so nice and sincere" or "personable and charming." All con artists seem that way. And remember, just because a charity advertises on radio and television doesn't mean it is legitimate and doesn't mean that someone has checked it out. It's also important to remember that hundreds of clergy, doctors, lawyers, and other supposed pillars of society have stolen millions of dollars from charities. In Pennsylvania two priests were charged with pocketing $1 million collected for a religious shrine. If a neighbor tells you that a particular charity is legitimate, ask, "How do you know this?" or "What are you basing this assessment on?"

- Never send cash or write out checks to individuals. Bypass the telemarketers and send a check directly to the charity. Do not give your credit card numbers or your Social Security number to solicitors. Do not promise checks or cash to a telephone solicitor who offers to send a courier to your door. Such solicitors are trying to rush you and are probably pocketing your contribution (and even if the hard sell is for a legitimate cause, $10 to $20 of your contribution will go to pay the courier). Don't be pressured into sending a contribution by overnight express.

  If a solicitor comes to your home, ask for identification (personal and organizational) and write this information down. For personal safety it is best not to invite the solicitor inside, especially if you are alone. It is smart to decide in advance how much money you can afford to give to charity. Do not donate out of guilt.

- If telemarketers are hounding you, tell them to put you on their legally required do-not-call list. If they call again, you can sue them in small-claims court. Kathy Chiero of Reynoldsburg, Ohio, filed a lawsuit because a telemarketer called her twice in one year, violating the Telephone Consumer Protection Act of 1991. "If they call once, they're making a living," said Chiero, as quoted in the *Arizona Republic*. "If they call again, they're making a mistake." She won a $500 judgment against the telemarketer.

The first time a charity calls, ask for a telephone number where the solicitor can be called back and also get a number for the headquarters of the organization to verify that it exists. At a news conference on July 8, 1995, Attorney General Janet Reno reported that illicit telephone pitches cost Americans $40 billion a year. Most experts say never to give money over the telephone unless you are 100 percent positive you know with whom you are dealing.

- Using similar-sounding names, many bogus charities are piggybacking on the reputations of well-known organizations. Insinuating that they represent legitimate established charities such as the Make-a-Wish Foundation, the American Cancer Society, or the National Multiple Sclerosis Society, enterprising con artists are making a fortune by giving their so-called charity a similar-sounding name. Children's Wish Foundation International, which was sued by the Connecticut attorney general for allegedly running a scam, is not the Make-a-Wish Foundation. The Multiple Sclerosis Foundation (which was sued for deceptive practices by the Connecticut attorney general's office) is not the National Multiple Sclerosis Society, which is highly acclaimed.

- Exchange suspicious sales pitch information with your friends, clubs, and organizations. One caller, claiming to represent a charity for the blind, casually told a 56-year-old woman, "Oh, just a minute, I dropped my pen—wait until my Seeing Eye dog finds it for me." When the woman mentioned this heartrending incident to her church group, four other women exclaimed, "He said the same thing to me!" Refusing to be victimized by the "sad, sad, story" tactic, the women investigated the charity and (with the help of the police) discovered that the "blind" solicitor drove to work in a new Mercedes Benz and donated the contributions to himself.

A crooked telemarketer claiming to represent the disabled said over and over again, "Excuse me a second while I wheel my chair a little closer to my desk." Police arrested the man during his morning jog but were unable to collect "over $200,000" he stole from well-meaning contributors. Clever business tycoons such as these (and there are thousands of them!) undermine the credibility of legitimate organizations that depend on the public's support.

- Keep in mind that anytime there is a local or national tragedy—the Oklahoma City bombing, a destructive hurricane, the murder of a police officer or firefighter—hundreds of scam artists scamper out of the woodwork to capitalize on people's sympathies. Voices of Freedom marketed bracelets purportedly so that Operation Desert Storm soldiers could phone home. This was a great cause to which most people would gladly contribute; the only problem was that all the donations were pocketed by crooks.

  Don't become cynical (most charities are genuine and good), but during times of national emergency and tragedy scrutinize fund-raising pitches very carefully, ask lots of questions . . . and then please give till it hurts.

- Don't fall for the "You won a prize" ruse used by phony charities and others. Crooked telemarketers are increasingly telling people that they have won a large amount of cash, a fancy car, jewelry, or other expensive prize.

But to collect the prize, you'll need to send a donation—often thousands of dollars—to a so-called charity. If the contributor receives any prize at all, it will usually be flowers, trinkets, or costume jewelry. Fast-talking salespeople might explain, "Your donation is needed to cover the federal taxes on your prize," or to cover so-called acquisition fees. One woman lost over $100,000 to this scam, and several other men and women have lost over $10,000. Nationwide, thousands of citizens, mostly elderly, are known to have been duped out of at least $12 million by telemarketers utilizing the "You won a prize" scheme. If a telemarketer tells you that you must send money to collect your prize, there is a 99.9 percent chance that you are dealing with a crook.

- The only thing worse than being conned once is to be conned twice. Don't fall victim to the "double con" tactic. Many people who have lost large sums of money to phony charities, the "You won a prize" tactic, and other scams have received follow-up calls from con artists who claim to be investigators with the attorney general's office or some other official-sounding organization. Pretending to be with the "financial fraud recovery section," these con artists or "reloaders" claim that they can recover all or most of the lost money. Naturally, the phony investigator requires a large fee—usually thousands of dollars—to be paid in advance. Throwing good money after bad, several thousand citizens were double conned in 1995 alone.

The names, addresses, and telephone numbers of people who have been conned by phony charities or who have generously contributed to legitimate charities are often put on so-called sucker lists. These lists of easy marks are then sold to a wide range of charities, con artists, fund-raisers, and telemarketers. Sad, but true.

- If you have been burned in the past or have suspicions about a particular charity, consider eliminating the middleman and giving your money directly to the needy party. "I used to give money to United Way," said a woman who was disgusted with the Aramony corruption scandal. "But now I find a struggling single mother or a needy child and write a check directly to them." By bypassing the bureaucracy, you can be assured that your money—all of your money—is going to the people for whom it was intended.

- The author has recorded hundreds of bogus charities and charities that have been sued and censored for deceptive and illegal practices. Most of these so-called charities had impressive-sounding names and appeared to be collecting for the most worthy of causes. Remember that many of these fraudulent groups select names similar to legitimate charities in order to confuse potential donors.

- Get involved, get angry, and get even. If you find you have been burned or suckered by a charity, don't stew in silence. Cracking down on charity fraud—or any type of white-collar crime—almost always begins with a complaint from an angry citizen. Help to root out the rot. Report the incident to your state's attorney general's office, to the financial fraud section of your local police, to a consumer protection agency, or to the Better Business Bureau. Politely ask what specifically the investigator intends to do with your complaint and call back at a later date to ask what action has been taken. Being ripped off is a punch in the nose, a stab in the heart, and a scar to the soul. Fight back. Don't allow anyone to treat you with such disrespect.

Contacts for charity information, complaints, and help include the following:

American Institute of Philanthropy
4579 Laclede Ave., Suite 136
St. Louis, MO 63108

Call For Action, Inc.
3400 Idaho Ave. NW, Suite 101
Washington, DC 20016
(202) 537-0585

National Charities Information Bureau
Dept. 414/ "Wise Giving Guide"
19 Union Square West, 6th Floor
New York, NY 10003-3395
(212) 929-6300

National Fraud Information Center Hotline
(800) 876-7060

Philanthropic Advisory Service
Council of Better Business Bureaus
4200 Wilson Blvd., Suite 800
Arlington, VA 22203-1804
(703) 276-0100

CHAPTER 5

Insurance Fraud

Patricia Latham, a 59-year-old kindergarten teacher with a history of slip-and-fall lawsuits, was videotaped frolicking at Walt Disney World after claiming to have lost the use of her hands in a fall; she had collected $15,000 from the Broward County, Florida, school system in the scam. Latham, who had won $500,000 from McDonald's in a suit stemming from a 1986 fall, sued a San Diego restaurant in 1989 under a different name and hired famed lawyer Melvin Belli to handle her case. She ran from the courtroom when her true identity was revealed.

In Jacksonville, Florida, two brothers persuaded Dr. John Rende, a dentist, to let them chop off his finger so that they could share $1.3 million in insurance money. When Dr. Rende changed his mind about cooperating, the brothers, Robert and Kenneth Alberton, forcibly held him down and cut off his right index finger. Dr. Rende collected a $1.3 million insurance payment because he was unable to practice dentistry and paid the Albertons $45,000. However, when the brothers became greedy and tried to extort an additional $500,000, Dr. Rende got scared and notified the FBI. After taping incriminating telephone conversations between the brothers and the dentist, the FBI arrested and charged the Alberton brothers.

These are just a few of the 9 million people in the United States who have defrauded insurance companies during the past decade. Thousands of these people have defrauded insurance companies at least 12 times and 900 are known to have defrauded insurance companies between 12 and 50 times. Making a full-time career of fraud, at least 237 people during the past decade have ripped off insurance companies 100 times or more.

Insurance fraud—property, casualty, and health—is a $95-billion-a-year scam nationwide. This is $95 billion that is stolen from the American consumer. This is $95,000,000,000 that the American consumer could be putting into savings accounts instead of giving it to crooks.

Some people stage phony burglaries and defraud their homeowners insurance company. Others, who really have been burglarized, exaggerate their claims. Some people stage automobile accidents and fabricate injuries. Others are involved in real accidents but lie about their disabilities; some burn buildings and homes or commit murders to collect insurance money.

Getting Rich Quick

As criminals are well aware, there are many tricks of the trade. Anyone who defrauds an insurance company *is* a criminal, and many of these criminals will go to almost any extreme in order to get rich quickly.

Hate Crimes and Arson for Insurance

Stooping to new lows, more than 80 people are believed to have concocted and staged hate crimes in order to collect insurance payments. Most of these people painted hate messages and then burned their own property.

On June 1, 1990, Joel Davis, a 47-year-old accountant and Jewish leader, was convicted of paying an oft-convicted felon to paint anti-Semitic signs on a Jewish summer resort and burn it down so that he could divert attention and collect on $400,000 in insurance claims. The felon also confessed that Davis had paid him $2500 a decade earlier to set fire to a private Orthodox Jewish school, saying that arson would be cheaper than renovation. The school had allegedly been targeted by anti-Semitic vandals shortly before the fire.

Adding to his problems, Davis also pleaded guilty to conspiring to murder an IRS agent who had been auditing his books. A white-collar criminal who used many different tactics to steal money, Davis was charged with owing $940,000 in back taxes.

Arson for insurance, one of the deadliest of white-collar crimes, costs society billions of dollars and hundreds of lives each year.

Every year arsonists burn office buildings, apartments, private homes, and a wide range of businesses in order to collect the insurance money.

Although many of these arsons are indeed committed by dark-hooded mafia thugs, more than 1500 arson-for-insurance cases each year are perpetrated by doctors, lawyers, teachers, business owners, and other so-called pillars of society.

In 26 known cases, arson for insurance has been committed by a priest, rabbi, minister, or monk.

The minister of a Methodist church in the state of Washington was charged on July 15, 1994, with setting a fire that destroyed his 70-year-old church. Authorities believe that Rev. Hutchins wanted to use the $500,000 to help replace another church that had also been destroyed by fire while he was pastor.

In Burlington, California, Paul Bray, a 32-year-old Seventh-Day Adventist pastor, confessed to setting a fire that destroyed his 60-year-old church in a scheme to collect the insurance money. The fire caused $1 million in damages to the wooden church.

Sign Up and Switch

Hundreds of white-collar criminals in recent years have used one of several "sign up and switch" scenarios to defraud insurance companies.

David Tully, 43, of Silver Spring, Maryland, pleaded guilty on June 30, 1995, to helping a roommate with AIDS get a life insurance policy by taking a physical in the roommate's name. When the roommate died, Tully, who was listed as the beneficiary, attempted to cash in the $730,000 life insurance policy.

Commenting on this case, an experienced insurance investigator stated: "Tully got caught, but I bet there are scores of people who used a similar tactic and collected the money."

James McElveen, 32, and Benny Milligan, 31, of Carville, Louisiana, also switched identities to defraud an insurance company.

When McElveen, who was uninsured, fell 30 feet from a waterfall and broke his back, his good friend, who was insured, switched identification cards with him in the emergency room so that McElveen could utilize Milligan's health insurance benefits.

Before the switch was discovered, McElveen had charged $41,107 to Milligan's U.S. government health insurance policy.

Milligan was sentenced to nine months in prison for the fraud and lost his job with Martin Marietta Corp., and McElveen was sentenced to seven months in prison.

Faking Death

"Faking death," explained a 58-year-old insurance executive from Massachusetts, "is another way people defraud insurance companies.

"We catch about a dozen people faking deaths each year," continued the executive. "But we assume a lot of people are successful with the scam and are never caught."

In one such case in Boston, a man tried unsuccessfully to collect on a $100,000 Aetna Casualty & Surety Insurance Co. policy which he had taken out on his brother after faking his brother's death. His brother, who is very much alive, was not even aware that the life insurance policy had been taken out.

Claiming that his brother had died of a heart attack in Haiti, the accused provided the insurance company with a bogus death certificate and photographs of what he said was a funeral.

Smelling a fraud, Aetna located the brother in a Boston suburb, refused to pay any money on the policy, and filed a lawsuit against the accused.

Recognizing Insurance Fraud

In a random sampling of 300 cases of insurance fraud, 121 cheats were caught (saving taxpayers millions of dollars) because concerned citizens reported their suspicions to the proper authorities. A 33-year-old bus driver who had allegedly hurt his back in an accident collected $126,000 in workers' compensation benefits. The driver's scam ended when a 61-year-old neighbor called the insurance fraud unit of her local police and reported that she had seen the man "digging his own backyard swimming pool and playing football with a bunch of rowdies."

As with most types of crime, there are often many witnesses to insurance fraud. Get involved. Concerned citizens with important information have prevented thousands of criminals from collecting insurance money for staged burglaries and slip-and-fall accidents, phony automobile injuries, arsons, and murder.

Churning

Be aware of a new form of deception the life insurance industry calls churning, which depletes the savings (known as cash value) you have built up in your old whole life policy. If an agent calls and says, "Hey, we have a way you can get more life insurance for little or no cost," be very suspicious.

In truth, a policy sold by a churner is very expensive and may leave you with no life insurance at all. A customer who accepts the churner's deal is actually taking a hidden loan against the cash value of the existing policy. In other words, the extra cost of the new policy is subtracted from the cash value of the old policy. When the cash value is used up—as has happened to many victims—your life insurance policy will lapse. Many spouses and family members who thought they were getting $100,000 to $200,000 in life insurance ended up with either a very small amount or nothing at all. A word to the wise: The phrase "nothing out of pocket" is generally a euphemism for churning.

Red Flags

The following red flags may indicate that you are being churned:

- You exchanged a small life insurance policy for a larger one and you are not paying much more.
- The agent claims that your new policy is free or does not involve any out-of-pocket costs.
- The agent may claim that the dividends on the old policy will pay the premiums on the new policy, for life.
- The agent, who may be with your current company or with a different company, claims that your old policy is no good, so you should switch immediately to a different policy.
- You received a notice from your insurance company telling you that you have loans on your policy that you didn't know you had. When you call to ask about these loans, your agent says, "Don't worry—it's just an internal paperwork thing," or "Just ignore it—it's a mistake."
- You get a notice that your policy has lapsed, and your agent again says, "Don't worry—that's a mistake."
- The policyholder is told that his or her spouse is entitled to a free policy. (The churner then diverts part of the policyholder's regular premium to pay for the

spouse's supposedly free policy. Loans are subsequently taken to keep the spouse's insurance policy active, until the original policy runs out of cash and lapses.)

Educating Yourself Against Churners

There are several things you can do to protect yourself against churners:

- Understand that you cannot get extra insurance, at a later age, for little or no additional cost.
- Understand that if your insurance company tells you that you have a loan or that your policy has lapsed, it's almost certainly true. Don't believe the agent who says "Don't worry."
- Do not sign a form that contains blanks or boxes that are left unchecked ("Don't worry about that space"), because the churner will fill in the blanks to his advantage.
- Insist on a letter that puts the claims in writing. A churner who misrepresents the facts usually does so verbally so that he can deny that he did something illegal. Insist that the letter be specific about loans, use of dividends, and whether cash values will be used to pay premiums. Does your coverage last until you are 100?

If you have already been victimized by a churner, write to the president of the company and to the state insurance department. If you are stonewalled, get a lawyer.

It is important to remember that it usually doesn't pay to replace an older cash-value policy or to use its cash value to increase your current coverage. Most experts advise that if you need more coverage you should add a policy rather than switch from the one you have.

Automobile Insurance Fraud

On May 24, 1995, FBI agents conducted raids in 31 states and arrested 126 people who had defrauded insurance companies by staging accidents, arsons, and thefts of motor vehicles. Agents had arrested an additional 328 suspects in previous months who had participated, organized, and trained people to stage accidents and fabricate injuries.

Dubbed Operation Sudden Impact, the FBI investigation and sting, which began in early 1994, was aimed at breaking up syndicates that defraud U.S. auto insurance companies and citizens out of $20 billion annually.

Staged, Paper, and Caused Accidents

Automobile accident fraud takes many different forms, but a high percentage of the scams fall into one of three categories:

- Staged accidents, in which cars and trucks with prior accident damage, or damage inflicted with sledge-hammers, are posed in such a way that they appear to have been involved in an accident.
- Paper accidents, in which no accident occurred but false accident reports are filed, sometimes with the assistance of corrupt police officers and body shop owners, to support insurance claims.
- Caused accidents, in which an innocent motorist is unwittingly forced into an accident for which he or she is technically liable.

Caused accidents, which some investigators refer to as the "swoop and squat" tactic, often involve the use of three cars to force an innocent driver into an accident that will appear to be his or her fault.

Conspirators utilizing the swoop and squat tactic will drive one car in front of the innocent driver while a second car pulls beside the unwitting target. Almost simultaneously, a third conspirator swoops in front of the lead car, which is expecting the move and slams on the brakes to feign avoiding the swerving car.

The innocent driver, in most cases, slams into the lead car from behind and is technically at fault for damages and the inevitable phony injuries. Purported victims in the lead car are then referred to one of a cadre of corrupt doctors for phony treatment and to crooked lawyers for legal advice.

Insurance fraud rings have purposely caused accidents with hundreds of tractor-trailers because the large trucks typically carry more liability insurance than passenger cars and are easier to force into an accident.

Sometimes, however, the staged accidents cause real injuries that are much more serious than the participants anticipated.

On June 17, 1992, in California, a truck-crash ring that recruited immigrants to fake injuries set up an accident with a huge car carrier on a Los Angeles freeway.

Swerving in front of the giant truck, the swoop and squat participants slammed on the brakes, causing the truck to overturn and crush the backseat of the setup car. Car passenger Jose Luis Lopez Perez, 29, a recent immigrant to the United States and a participant in the setup, was crushed to death.

Four months later, after an extensive investigation into the crash, police arrested attorney Gary P. Miller, 44, an alleged mastermind of the ring, and charged him with murder. Filemon Santiago, 23, whom police believe was a recruiter for the ring, and Jorge Sanchez, 30, the driver of the vehicle that was crushed, were also charged with murder.

In addition to the fatal car carrier crash, authorities charged attorney Miller with four other truck wrecks and linked him to a freeway crash with a car, several wrecks on streets, and one fake accident that occurred only on paper. Investigators said that Miller paid Santiago and others from $500 to $1000 for each phony accident that they brought to his law practice.

Miller reportedly visited Lopez Perez's widow after the fatal crash and offered to file a wrongful death suit against the innocent driver of the car carrier.

Sadly, there isn't a city in the United States that does not have an automobile insurance fraud problem, and there isn't a single motorist who doesn't pay a price for this fraud.

Accident fraud costs each American household more than $210 annually in higher premiums, and with every new fraudulent claim, innocent drivers will have to reach even deeper into their pockets. As the crooks get richer, the honest citizens get poorer.

The massive automobile insurance fraud problem has become a dangerous and hugely expensive epidemic. In fact, a study by the Western Insurance Industry Service found that up to 25 percent of the 570,000 accidents that it surveyed were staged.

Recognizing Auto Insurance Scams

Recognize that you've been invited to become a participant in fraud if someone suggests that a certain lawyer or doctor can help you make a lot of money from an automobile accident. Understand that if a body shop offers to inflate your damage estimate you are participating in insurance fraud.

Be careful not to purchase a stolen vehicle. It's best to

buy from a licensed dealer. Always check the vehicle identification number for alterations or replacement. Be suspicious of fresh paint jobs, remade keys, or the absence of a title or registration. Be suspicious if you need a different key to open different doors on the car.

If you are involved in or witness an accident, report it to the proper authorities and volunteer to help investigators and to testify in court if there is evidence of fraud. Please report a fraud if you are aware of one. You can call the local police, the attorney general's office, state insurance regulators, or the National Insurance Crime Bureau (NICB) at 1-800-835-6422.

Dishonest Insurance Agents

When most people think of insurance fraud, they conjure up images of staged accidents, phony slip-and-falls, and workers' compensation scams. However, hundreds of millions of dollars each year are stolen by insiders—insurance company owners, executives, agents, and adjusters. Theft by insiders has devastating consequences for consumers and society.

Fraud by Insiders

On August 17, 1994, in Philadelphia, Louis E. Silver, 30, an insurance consultant, was found guilty of 145 counts of mail fraud after he sold nonexistent health insurance to several companies.

Silver, a trusted insurance representative, pocketed more than $500,000 that hundreds of hardworking union employees had paid him for health insurance. Dozens of workers were saddled with backbreaking medical bills after being hospitalized for illnesses and injuries.

A similar health insurance scam affecting 1350 families and individuals occurred in Charlotte, North Carolina.

In that case, a federal grand jury charged six officers of CAP Programs, Inc., with stealing $21 million that workers from 120 small businesses had paid for health insurance. Instead of purchasing health insurance with the money, the officers allegedly pocketed the premiums to buy lavish homes, luxury cars, and beachfront condominiums.

One worker did not discover that his health insurance policy was worthless until he had a heart transplant operation and was shouldered with $200,000 in medical bills.

The indictment said that the dishonest CAP officers told customers that their medical bills would be covered by the Travelers Insurance Co., but Travelers Insurance Co. was only responsible for processing the claims.

Although it was of little consolation to the victims, the accused executives got a small taste of what it is like to be victimized. Law enforcement officials swooped down and seized seven homes, 26 luxury vehicles, and personal and business bank accounts worth $3 million from the six defendants.

Some dishonest insurance executives seem to have learned a few tricks from dishonest lawyers.

In Virginia Beach, Virginia, on April 27, 1995, police charged a 49-year-old insurance agent with forging a 93-year-old woman's $5 million will a few months before she died, in an attempt to defraud the woman and her survivors of money and property.

The indictment also accused the insurance agent of forging a deed so that he would inherit, among other assets, the woman's $350,000 condominium apartment.

Fortunately, two supposed witnesses whose signatures

were forged on the will testified in court that the document was a phony.

The insurance agent, who had been advising the woman on financial matters, was well aware that she had $4.5 million in a Merrill Lynch account and owned $800,000 worth of real estate.

Like most white-collar criminals, dishonest insurance agents frequently target the elderly. In fact, during 1995 alone, insurance professionals in the United States cheated older adults out of at least $380 million.

Steven D. Thomas, 37, of Gloucester, New Jersey, was sentenced to four years in prison for pocketing more than $175,000 in life and automobile insurance premiums from about 100 customers. His victims included an elderly blind woman who paid him $136,000 in life insurance premiums and discovered her policy was worthless.

Dishonest insurance agents, like dishonest lawyers, are often difficult to catch because as experts in their field they know a hundred different ways to steal.

On June 5, 1995, in Santa Barbara, California, insurance agent Devin Charles Park, 36, was sentenced to 63 months in jail and ordered to pay $4 million in restitution for stealing funds from two title insurance companies that he managed.

Exploiting his position as president, Park had forged signatures and stolen customers' escrow funds—money held as collateral in special bank accounts—and used the money for a lavish lifestyle and to purchase country club memberships, stocks, bonds, and other personal items.

Robert J. Keller, the former executive of two insurance agencies in Hawaii, used the millions of dollars that he stole from policyholders to purchase Porsches, Mercedes Benzes, expensive artwork, jewelry, and luxury hotel accommodations.

"You can imagine how thrilled we were to learn that good news," joked a policyholder who lives in Hawaii and California.

Using a wide range of techniques to steal money, Keller pocketed premiums paid by policyholders, selfishly refused to pay claims in order to keep the money for himself, and stole in excess of $6 million in accounts receivable, including $1 million in cash.

Keller's greed cost Hawaii's two largest automobile insurance agencies an incredible $17 million in losses. He was eventually sentenced to three years in prison for his conviction on insurance fraud and income tax evasion, but that was a very light punishment considering the harm he did.

Limited only by their imaginations and the access that their positions allow, dishonest insurance agents have literally scores of accounts from which they can embezzle money.

In Florida an insurance adjuster was charged with stealing $326,178 in damage settlements from Hurricane Andrew victims. Authorities said that he forged the signatures of hurricane victims on claim checks and simply deposited the money in his personal checking account.

In Pennsylvania, Sidney M. Baer, a multimillionaire insurance broker, pleaded guilty to cheating his clients out of $466,573. He had pocketed refunds that were meant for his large corporate clients.

In Arizona, insurance agent Robert Chrysler Morgan was forced to pay $134,000 and surrender his license for defrauding thousands of customers. Morgan illegally charged 2500 people a $15 fee when they applied for insurance, pocketed hundreds of refunds owed to his customers, and charged 841 people $65 apiece for auto-club memberships after telling them that the membership was a necessary part of the policy.

Uninsured Drivers

The actions of some crooked insurance agents not only deplete customers' bank accounts, but also endanger life and limb by allowing dangerous, uninsured motorists to continue driving.

On June 4, 1995, state and local police in Los Angeles arrested 46 suspects who were involved in an auto insurance fraud ring that arranged for uninsured drivers who had car accidents to obtain backdated insurance policies.

In order to line their pockets, the suspected ringleaders were providing uninsured motorists with auto insurance policies backdated to a few days before the date of their car accidents so that the drivers could file claims for damages and injuries.

The insurance kept dangerous drivers on the road, and the illegal claims, which ranged from $1000 to over $35,000, cost insurance companies $410,000, a sum that did not include what insurance companies paid to investigate the fraud.

Investigators made another interesting discovery when they searched the house of one of the suspects. They found more than 50 weapons, including M-16s, an Uzi submachine gun, and explosive devices. They also learned that he was on probation for carrying a concealed weapon.

Robert A. Lassen, a 49-year-old insurance executive from Maryland, also found a way to get rich while encouraging unsafe drivers to stalk the highways.

On March 7, 1994, Lassen was sentenced to eight years in prison for writing more than 700 bogus high-risk automobile insurance policies and keeping $500,000 in premiums for himself. Instead of applying the money to an insurance policy for his customers, Lassen was using the money to pay college tuition for his children, pay off personal loans, and join a country club.

Meanwhile, several of Lassen's high-risk customers, who were apparently frustrated demolition-derby contestants, were banging up cars on the interstate and filing claims on their nonexistent insurance policies.

"Well, at least that bastard got eight years in prison," said a 74-year-old Annapolis, Maryland, woman who was ripped off by another agent. No one had the heart to tell her the reality of the criminal justice system: The "bastard" will actually serve less than two years.

If insurance industry leaders expect to put an end to the costly problem of fraud, they will first have to look inward and put their own house in order.

Exposing the Insiders

Implementing stricter internal controls, insurance companies need to put an end to embezzlement by employees and pass the savings on to the customers.

On July 20, 1995, in Madison, Wisconsin, Carol Lampien, 60, a claims service representative, pleaded guilty to embezzling $498,970 from her employer, Wausau Insurance Co. Lampien, unfortunately, was only one of hundreds of employees who have embezzled money from insurance companies in the United States. Focusing on fraudulent claims, many insurance companies have turned a blind eye to the dishonest employee. If more insurance companies would look inward and use more of their investigative resources to catch embezzlers, every consumer would save at least $50 per year on insurance payments.

Sometimes it takes a lawsuit to keep an insurance company honest. If you think you have been cheated out of a legitimate claim, don't be afraid to hire a lawyer and fight for your rights.

Norman Jensen, a 52-year-old musician, purchased what he thought was a major health insurance policy from Transport Life Insurance Co. after a telephone solicitor called his home. Brochures describing the policy offered Jensen a lifetime maximum of $1 million and appeared to offer coverage for surgery, hospital and home care, doctor visits, and private nursing and outpatient services. But after Jensen developed cancer, he was dismayed to learn that his policy covered only $3400 out of $47,000 in medical bills.

Feeling he was being cheated, Jensen sued Transport Life Insurance Co. and won. Agreeing that Jensen had been defrauded and misled, a Los Angeles Superior Court jury awarded Jensen $25 million in punitive damages. The jury apparently wanted the high punitive damages to act as a deterrent so that other insurance companies would not defraud their customers.

Insurance companies are obligated to honor their policies. If you are one of thousands of people each year who are ripped off by an insurance company, your only option is to stand up and fight for your rights.

First Families of Fraud

The Kallao Clan

Working a deal with an insured homeowner in Cincinnati, Thomas Kallao used sandpaper to scrape his knees and then contended that the homeowner's Labrador retriever knocked him down a long flight of stairs. The fall, he claimed, caused a concussion, abrasions, chipped teeth, and other injuries. Nationwide Insurance settled the claim for $39,450. Thomas Kallao kept $37,450 for himself and his family, gave the cooperative homeowner about $2000, and, we would hope, rewarded the Labrador retriever with a thick sirloin steak.

Curtis Kallao, another member of the so-called First Family of Fraud, poured antifreeze on the ground and intentionally slipped and fell at a gas station in Indianapolis. Convincingly claiming that he had broken his nose, chipped two teeth, and sustained neck and back injuries, Curtis Kallao collected over $22,000 from American States Insurance. One can imagine that the exuberant Kallao clan, celebrating yet another of many windfalls, cashed the check, laughed uproariously, toasted each other with drink, and boasted of past successes.

The celebration, however, ended on June 30, 1993, in a Chicago courtroom, when the Kallao family—husbands and wives, fathers and sons, sisters and brothers, aunts and uncles—pleaded guilty to scores of staged accidents and admitted that they had cheated insurance companies out of $500,000 since 1987.

Specializing in fake automobile crashes and slip-and-fall accidents, the Kallaos, using false IDs and aliases, claimed phony injuries in Chicago, Las Vegas, Detroit, Phoenix, Cincinnati, Indianapolis, and other cities.

Defrauding insurance companies was a full-time job for the Kallao clan. "When most people went to work in the morning," said an Illinois investigator, "the Kallaos were holding a family conference and rehearsing their next staged accident."

After years of practice, various members of the Kallao family became convincing actors. One member of the clan boasted that hospital personnel stuck a tube in his stomach to check for internal injuries because he had feigned such excruciating pain. Another laughed about the time an ambulance crew strapped him to a stretcher in the mistaken belief that he had a broken back.

Many of the accidents the Kallaos staged seemed extremely realistic because the pain was real. Thomas Kallao once intentionally cut his forehead with a razor blade and asked a friend to punch him repeatedly in the nose so that a fake fall in the friend's home would look realistic. State Farm Insurance paid Kallao $15,000 for the act.

Once a slip-and-fall specialist has a broken nose he will feign broken noses over and over again because it is difficult to tell a fresh break from an old one.

The court learned that the Kallaos would walk into stores, restaurants, and offices, pour shampoo or another liquid on the floor and then, with great fanfare, fall down and claim a soft-tissue or other injury that is virtually impossible to verify medically.

To stage car accidents, the Kallaos would drive to an isolated area and ram two cars together until they had created the desired effect. They would then pick up any parts that fell off, pack the vehicles with supposed victims, locate an ideal location for an accident, and pose the vehicles to appear as if there had been a high-speed rear-end collision.

At that point, the "victims" would prick their skin with pins or razor blades, smear themselves with blood, call an ambulance, and start moaning and groaning.

Sometimes the Kallaos employed "inside" help; they set up several falls and car accidents with the assistance of Lawrence Hogden, an insurance agent and adjuster who enlisted the help of Herb Breidel, a senior State Farm Insurance employee. These connections provided the First Family of Fraud with some of their grandest victories.

In a staged two-car crash that occurred in Peoria, Illinois, in 1991, Hogden claimed to have rear-ended a Mercedes that was packed with six members of the Kallao family—Thomas, David, Eugene, Agnes, Curtis, and Steven—all of whom pretended to suffer soft-tissue injuries.

It was no coincidence that the claims were assigned to a young State Farm adjuster who just happened to be supervised by Breidel. Every time the adjuster suggested a sum of money to settle the claim, Breidel gave her unsolicited permission to offer the "injured" parties a higher amount. Breidel then told Thomas Kallao and Hogden the maximum amount that the unwitting adjuster was allowed to offer them.

In this case, the Kallaos received a settlement totaling $137,696. Breidel, the crooked insurance agent, reportedly received 10 to 15 percent of the money.

Unfortunately, it is not unusual to find entire families involved in insurance fraud. In fact, thousands of family groups, including husbands and wives, brothers and sisters, parents and children, conspire to defraud insurance companies every year.

The Ballog Bunch

On June 27, 1995, David Ballog, 60, the patriarch of a family that bilked $758,000 from insurance companies, was sentenced to 20 months in prison. In the six months prior to his sentencing, 10 other members of the Ballog family were convicted of fraud—including his wife, three sons, a daughter-in-law, and a grandson, David Ballog III, who had been making phony claims since he was seven.

Ballog, who was related through marriage to the Kallao

family, apparently didn't believe that there was honor among thieves. Soon after the Kallao clan was arrested in 1993, Ballog turned himself in to police because he felt that it was only a matter of time before someone in the Kallao family offered to inform on him in exchange for a lighter sentence. A compulsive gambler, Ballog was also trying to escape the clutches of a violent, mob-connected bookmaker to whom he owed money.

By cooperating with police, Ballog received a lighter sentence and the insurance industry learned a bit more about criminal deception.

The Ballogs, the police learned, would draw blood from their arms with syringes and spread it on their mouths and noses after supposedly falling, and frequently stuffed cotton in their mouths and noses to make their faces appear swollen.

To create hazardous conditions in more than 100 hotels, restaurants, and offices, Ballog and his family poured oil on floors, stuffed towels in toilets to make them overflow, and separated U-joints on sinks to cause leakages.

The Ballogs even concocted their own homemade vomit to slip on, made from Thousand Island salad dressing, mashed potatoes, and other colorful and gooey ingredients.

Giving new meaning to the saying that "every cloud has a silver lining," the Ballogs always found a way to exploit real injuries. One family member, for example, suffered a compression fracture of his vertebrae in the early 1980s in a legitimate fall. But since evidence of that injury still showed up on X rays, he staged 17 phony falls and bilked 17 insurance companies for his compression fracture in the 1990s.

On occasion, the Ballogs would work with a corrupt police officer or detective.

In 1987, the Ballogs recruited Chicago Police Detective Fred Pascente to help them with an insurance fraud scheme.

Pascente told his insurance company that he was walking by a local playground when he saw a 16-year-old boy acting cocky as he played sandlot football with his buddies. Deciding to teach the youngster a lesson, Pascente, then 45, said he charged onto the field and tackled the youth, badly hurting the boy's knee. The boy needed two operations to correct the damage.

Sorry about his actions, Pascente took responsibility for the injury and reported the incident to his insurance company.

Posing as the boy's uncle, David Ballog negotiated a $112,328 settlement with the insurance company and shared the money with Pascente and others.

In a Chicago courtroom on November 7, 1994, Pascente confessed to authorities and insurance adjusters what really happened that day in 1987:

The boy did have a bad knee, but it had been injured weeks earlier in a football game. Detective Pascente never tackled the boy, and Ballog was not the boy's uncle. The insurance company was bilked out of a whopping $112,328 by a clever and corrupt group of con artists.

Between 1987 and 1994, Ballog and his cohorts filed over 100 false claims in 16 states.

Murder for Insurance

When Anthony Riggs, a 22-year-old Persian Gulf war veteran, was shot to death in front of his in-laws' home shortly after returning from the war, it was assumed that the soldier was another tragic victim of a Detroit street robbery. Police soon learned, however, that the victim's wife and brother-in-law conspired to murder Riggs in order to collect his $175,000 life insurance policy.

People who rationalize that insurance fraud is a nonviolent crime are obviously naive about the reality of life and the dark side of human nature. In the real world hundreds of people are killed each year in arson and murder-for-insurance plots, and many of these cases shock even the most callous of investigators.

Frannie Hannon Snite, a special-education teacher from Greenville, South Carolina, was convicted of attempting to murder her husband on their honeymoon. She beat him repeatedly with a tire iron in hopes of collecting a $1.4 million life insurance policy. David Crist, 36, from Baltimore, Maryland, was arraigned on charges of pushing his nine-year-old deaf daughter in front of a truck to collect a $58,000 life insurance policy. The man hired to drive over the girl told police he could not go through with the scheme and swerved his truck at the last second to avoid hitting her. On August 20, 1995, in Monroeville, Alabama, Stanley Kidd was convicted of murdering his twin 14-month-old daughters so that he could avoid paying $806 a month in child support and collect on a $16,000 life insurance policy.

Domestic Violence

Murder-for-insurance plots have also become an integral, but largely unpublicized, aspect of the domestic violence problem in the United States. More than 75 percent of the murder-for-insurance plots recorded each year involve spouses, lovers, and family members killing one another. Some family members do their own killing; others hire someone else to do it.

John J. Chew, an unemployed New Jersey roofer, took out an expensive $250,000 insurance policy on his girlfriend, 29-year-old Teresa Bowman, and listed himself as the beneficiary. Chew, 44, was charged with murder after Ms. Bowman was found with her throat slashed in a parking lot at a Hilton hotel. Chew's own sister testified that she gave him a ride home from the Hilton on the day of the murder.

In Cook County, Illinois, a jury convicted Kevin Miller, 22, of murdering Catherine Garner, 28, with a shotgun as Mrs. Garner returned from a trick-or-treat outing with her two-year-old son. Miller and the victim's estranged husband, Charles David Garner, 26, were involved in a scheme to collect $250,000 in life insurance proceeds.

On May 30, 1995, in New City, New York, a court sentenced 24-year-old Michelle Lennon to 20 years to life in prison for murdering her husband, Brooke Lennon, a 54-year-old senior vice president for the Grand Union supermarket chain in Wayne, New Jersey. Prosecutors said that she committed the murder to collect on a $2 million life insurance policy and the $280,000 her husband had in the bank.

Mrs. Lennon, who never showed any remorse for her crime or her greed, admitted that she beat her husband with a baseball bat, placed a plastic bag over his head, and then strangled him with a telephone cord. She and her lover, a 25-year-old unemployed motorcycle repairman, then placed Mr. Lennon in the trunk of his company-leased Lincoln Continental Mark VIII and disposed of the body in a nearby woods.

Cover-Ups

"Nobody knows how many victims of supposed street robberies and home invasions are actually pawns in life insurance plots," said a senior New York City police investigator, "but my gut feeling is that the number is quite large and that an awful lot of people get away with it."

It is known that, in recent years, at least 23 murders that were made to look like everyday street crimes were later found to be sophisticated murder-for-insurance schemes.

Melvin Thompson, a 49-year-old transmission shop owner, was shot to death shortly before 7:00 P.M. on June 14, 1990, as he was about to close his service shop on Santa Monica Boulevard in Los Angeles. The killer also stole an undetermined amount of cash and the Rolex watch on Thompson's wrist.

Since there had been a series of Rolex robberies in Los Angeles, police initially assumed that Thompson was another victim of this trend. After all, only one week earlier, a 42-year-old man was shot in his newly purchased Beverly Hills home by a gunman who had spotted the victim's expensive Rolex and followed him.

But bit by bit, investigators grew more suspicious of Catherine Thompson, the victim's wife.

"There were four pieces of evidence that suggested his wife might be involved," said a Los Angeles Police Department investigator familiar with the case.

"One—a guy named Phil Sanders was seen driving from the shop shortly after the shooting," the investigator explained.

"Two—Sanders and Mrs. Thompson had been involved in some sort of real estate scam together." That interesting coincidence, which netted Mrs. Thompson and Sanders about $100,000, was viewed with great curiosity by police.

"Three—the Rolex watch that was supposedly stolen in the robbery was found in Thompson's home when we searched there." Suddenly, the Rolex robbery theory that even Mrs. Thompson espoused was no longer a possibility.

"Four," the detective continued, "good ole Mrs. Thompson was the beneficiary of her husband's $400,000 life insurance policy.

"Excuse my cynicism," the investigator deadpanned, "but that kind of money has tempted a lot of people to forget their marriage vows."

On September 28, 1992, a jury in Los Angeles put these and other pieces of the puzzle together and sentenced Catherine Thompson to death for contracting Phillip Sanders to murder her husband.

In order to add a touch of realism to phony street robberies and home invasions, some murder-for-insurance schemers, like Dan Montecalvo, 49, of Pasadena, California, have wounded themselves. After shooting his wife twice, Montecalvo wounded himself in the back so that police would think the assailant was a panicked burglar. Several church friends said Montecalvo was a "good guy," but police discovered that he was desperately in debt and spent most of his time hustling women in bars. He was convicted of murdering his wife of nine years in an attempt to collect on her $600,000 life insurance policy.

Multiple Murder Attempts

"I sure can't help but wonder how many people get away with these murders," said an LAPD investigator. He also guessed that the number was quite large.

In at least a dozen known cases, people trying to collect on life insurance policies have tenaciously tried to kill their target five, six, and even ten times before finally being successful.

The deceptively charming 58-year-old Lucia Bravo, of Los Angeles, California, was one of those tenacious killers.

Trying to collect on five life insurance policies worth $700,000, Mrs. Bravo attempted to kill her husband, Miguel Bravo, who was 16 years her junior, on six occasions before finally shooting him—or having him shot—twice in the head at point-blank range on July 26, 1991. She then had her loving husband buried in the cheapest casket that money could buy.

Poor Miguel, who never suspected his charming wife, always assumed that his would-be assassins were somehow associated with the people to whom he owed money.

Thanks to the work of Los Angeles Police Detective Lawrence Garrett and an insurance investigator who wanted to make sure a man named Miguel Bravo had actually been killed, Lucia Bravo was convicted of her husband's murder on April 7, 1995.

Perhaps the scariest finding, in a sampling of almost 1000 murder-for-insurance cases, was the discovery that at least 46 individuals were convicted or strongly suspected of killing more than one spouse, lover, or family member for the insurance money.

"One woman buried ten husbands," said an FBI agent stationed in Washington, D.C., "and she has turned quite blond with grief.

"To my knowledge she has only been convicted of one murder," the agent continued, "but the other nine deaths are highly suspicious . . . and she made money on each of them."

Three befuddling trends that leave most people just shaking their heads are the cases in which children kill their parents, adults kill children, or one parent teams up with a child to kill the other parent.

"I've seen all three of these combinations so often I'm no longer shocked," said a detective in Atlanta, Georgia, "and that really bothers me."

White-Collar Killers

"When most people think of life insurance fraud they usually envision some drooling, unemployed lowlife, . . . but the four cases I've encountered were all professionals," said a successful 56-year-old insurance executive from Chevy Chase, Maryland.

The executive's experience is in keeping with the national data. A high percentage of the proven murder-for-insurance cases each year involve lawyers, medical personnel, business executives, and other professionals.

In recent years, two highly publicized and sensational cases involving a doctor and a lawyer occurred in California and Georgia.

Dr. Richard Boggs, a 57-year-old California neurologist, was sentenced to life in prison in 1992 for his part in a complex and cold-blooded insurance scheme that involved murdering a patient and then giving the victim someone else's identity.

Dr. Boggs lured Ellis Henry Greene, 32, into his office, disabled him with six stun guns he had purchased three months earlier and then suffocated him.

The good doctor then called paramedics and falsely identified the dead patient as Melvin Eugene Hanson. The real Melvin Hanson, who in 1992 was charged with co-conspiracy with Dr. Boggs, was very much alive and owned a $1.5-million life insurance policy, which the two conspirators had apparently hoped to share.

Lawyer Fredric Tokars, a prominent Atlanta, Georgia,

prosecutor and part-time judge, was convicted April 8, 1994, of arranging the murder of his wife, who was shot to death in front of the couple's two young sons.

Sara Tokars, 39, a Farrah Fawcett look-alike, and her sons, then four and six, were kidnapped from their Atlanta home after returning from a Thanksgiving trip to Florida. The gunman forced the three hostages into Mrs. Tokars' car and ordered her to drive off. After driving less than a mile, the assailant shot Mrs. Tokars in the head and ran from the car. The children fled, crying and confused, to a nearby house.

Living in an expensive suburban home, the Tokarses appeared to enjoy a perfect, picture-book lifestyle. The beautiful Mrs. Tokars, by all accounts a doting and loving mother and wife, energetically attended to her sons' activities and her husband's career. Already a successful lawyer, Fredric Tokars had political ambitions and investments in several Atlanta nightclubs. The couple appeared to be successful and happy.

However, appearances can be deceiving. Police soon learned that Mrs. Tokars had twice visited divorce lawyers and had even hired a private detective who was instructed—ominously—to turn his findings over to the police if anything happened to her.

Police also learned that Tokars, the prominent lawyer, was part of a cocaine trafficking enterprise that operated out of Atlanta, Detroit, and Miami, and pushed drugs and drug money through nightclubs and at least 21 corporations.

Mrs. Tokars had uncovered her husband's criminal activities, and with the divorce pending he was apparently afraid she might talk.

Tokars, who conveniently insured his wife for a cool $1.7 million, simply made the cold and calculated business decision to have her killed.

Over the years the insurance industry has lost hundreds of millions of dollars as a result of murder-for-insurance schemes.

Although many of the perpetrators are caught, experts estimate that there are thousands of beneficiaries who are currently sipping champagne, nibbling at caviar, thumbing their noses at the law, and grieving all the way to the bank.

If you suspect someone is plotting a murder-for-insurance scheme, the best thing you can do is call the police immediately.

Tips for Fighting Back

- If you are a witness or victim of insurance fraud, get involved and report it.

- Don't get caught in the middle of an auto insurance scheme. Know how to tell if the used car you are buying might be stolen.

- If you think you have been cheated out of a legitimate claim, don't be afraid to hire a lawyer. If you are one of thousands of people each year who are ripped off by an insurance company, your only option is to stand up and fight for your rights.

- Be on the lookout for phony insurance agents. Scores of impostor insurance salesmen in recent years have pocketed premiums for liability, health, automobile, life, and other types of insurance and have victimized thousands of businesses and individuals who attempted to collect on nonexistent policies. Recognizing that many white-collar criminals have impersonated insurance agents, consumers should first determine that the salesman has a license and then check the status of the policy directly with the insurance company.

- Know how to spot a churner. Understand that you cannot get extra insurance, at a later age, for little or no additional cost. If you are approached with a churner's sales pitch, insist on a letter that puts the claims in writing.

- Don't be fooled into thinking that all insurance fraud crimes are nonviolent. There are scores of incidents of people being murdered for insurance payoffs.

For more information, to get help, or to report an insurance crime, you can call your local police, the attorney general's office, your state insurance regulators, or the National Insurance Crime Bureau (NICB) at 1-800-835-6422.

CHAPTER 6

The Religious Ruse

Religion in the United States is a big, big business that generates big, big money. And wherever there is money there's temptation.

Religious institutions in the United States—more than 130,000 separate places of worship—collect approximately $58 billion in donations each year.

But donations represent only one part of the total revenue brought in by churches, synagogues, mosques, and temples. Most religious institutions also generate money through investments.

In 1991 the *New York Times* reported that the Mormon Church collects at least $4.3 billion a year from its members and generates an additional $4 billion a year from investments and companies owned by the Mormon Church.

The *New York Times* reported in 1993 that the secretive and controversial Church of Scientology, which has won its battle for federal tax exemption, counts assets of about

$400 million and takes in another $300 million a year from counseling fees, book sales, and investments.

Critics assert that Scientology is a sham religion dedicated more to financial benefit than to spiritual salvation—and they like to point out that the church's 440-foot yacht, the *Freewinds*, is valued at $15.2 million.

Each year in the United States a wide range of criminals—including thousands of dishonest clergy and employees of religious institutions—steal more than $14 billion from God's purse.

The money is stolen, siphoned off, and swindled in a hundred different ways.

Jim Bakker and Tammy Faye

Who could forget Jim Bakker, the former television evangelist who bilked 118,000 of his loyal PTL followers out of an incredible $158 million? Using the money his parishioners had invested in Heritage USA, a 2300-acre Christian theme park, preacher Bakker purchased expensive homes, cars, and jewelry for himself and his wife Tammy Faye.

Adding to the hypocrisy, Bakker engaged in a scandalous affair with sexy church secretary Jessica Hahn and then diverted $265,000 of church money to buy her silence.

Hahn talked, despite the bribe, and turned sex and sin into some really big money; she was reportedly paid $1 million to pose nude for *Playboy* magazine and earned additional money to star in the video *Jessica Hahn Bares It All.*

· It's safe to assume that PTL (Praise The Lord or People That Love) has been very good to Jessica Hahn's career.

After serving only 4½ years in a white-collar prison for stealing *$158,000,000*, Bakker was released in 1994. He was originally sentenced to 45 years in prison, but that time was reduced to eight years after an appeals court ruled that the sentencing judge improperly injected religious views.

Tammy Faye divorced her incarcerated husband in 1992, after 30 years of marriage, and married multimillionaire church builder Roe Messner in 1993. Messner and Jim Bakker were former partners in the PTL ministry business.

As the facade was removed from the Praise The Lord ministry, like makeup from Tammy Faye's face, followers were left staring at something scary and unrecognizable; parishioners could now see that PTL also stood for Pass The Loot.

Religious-related investment swindles, run by false prophets, fleece the faithful out of an additional $250 million each year.

Jimmy Swaggart and Other "Affinity Frauds"

In what is often dubbed "affinity fraud," pious con artists pass themselves off as members of a particular religious group and then exploit that group's beliefs to gain confidence and life savings.

Advertising on Christian radio stations, a Washington state company sold $55 million of high-risk debt securities to an estimated 7000 investors. When the company filed for bankruptcy, the investors learned that it had no connection to their church, their goals, or their religious beliefs.

Bad advice, much of which borders on the criminal, also takes its toll on religious coffers.

In 1993, the Westchester Jewish Center in Mamaroneck, New York, claimed that it lost $650,000 after being misled by a Wall Street brokerage firm. Synagogue officials charged that the broker claimed that mortgage-backed securities known as collateralized mortgage obligations, or CMOs, were safe when, in fact, they are considered risky and highly speculative.

The more than 100 religious organizations that invested money in the Foundation for New Era Philanthropy (see Chapter 4) lost many millions of dollars when the so-called charitable organization filed for bankruptcy in 1995.

Two well-paid religious leaders who served as middlemen for New Era and convinced many churches to invest $20 million in the first six months of 1995 alone are being investigated by both state and federal law enforcement authorities.

But most of the $14 billion stolen from religious organizations each year is embezzled by trusted employees, high-ranking officials, and even clergy.

On August 10, 1995, in Bethesda, Maryland, Lester Kaplan, the 48-year-old executive director of the Jewish Community Center of Greater Washington, pleaded guilty to embezzling $1 million from the Jewish organization.

Working in cahoots with three other officials (the chief financial officer, a bookkeeper, and a building superintendent) Kaplan and his three coconspirators siphoned off $1 million that they claimed was being spent on cleaning and other services.

"In truth, we don't know where our money is going or what those characters are spending it on," said a 38-year-old California woman who was suckered into giving $500 to evangelist Jimmy Swaggart in 1990.

"I forgave Swaggart when he was caught with a prostitute in 1988," said the California woman. "But when he got caught again in '91 I couldn't help but wonder if he was using my money."

On October 11, 1991, the infamous Jimmy Swaggart was issued three traffic tickets in Indio, California, for driving his Jaguar on the wrong side of the road, driving an unregistered vehicle, and not wearing a seat belt. A prostitute riding with Swaggart when he was stopped said that he had a collection of pornographic magazines with him and had picked her up for sex.

Recognizing the Affinity Frauds

Face up to the facts. Many religious groups sound divine but are actually devilish. Each year in the United States a wide range of criminals, crazies, and con artists—including thousands of dishonest clergy and employees of religious institutions—steal more than $14 billion in God's name. Are most clergy and most religious organizations legitimate and honest? Absolutely! But people who believe that all such organizations are good are the individuals most likely to be financially victimized.

Parishioners should question whether clerics are the best people to invest their money. From January 1989 to January 1996, clerics claiming to be financial consultants cheated over 1.6 million people out of their savings.

Be careful when you award power of attorney to anyone—including your priest, rabbi, or minister; more than 220 clergy, real and phony, are known to have criminally abused this legal document. In 1995, police in Florida arrested Rev. John Canning, 58, a pastor of the multidenominational Fountain of Life Church, and charged him with the murders of Leo and Hazel Gleese. The 90-year-old couple were killed after they discovered that Rev. Canning had abused the power of attorney they had given him and had allegedly stolen tens of thousands of dollars from their bank accounts. Before giving someone carte blanche power over your finances, implement protective checks and balances.

Be very specific, not general, concerning the powers you are granting. If you give your minister the power to pay your bills, be very specific as to which bills will be paid. Put a limit on how much money can be spent in a given month. Do not be rushed into signing any document, and always have a trusted third party review the agreement. Always ask yourself, "How might this document be abused?" Without becoming cynical, understand that some clergy are crooks. Just because someone has the title of minister, rabbi, or priest does not guarantee that that person is honest or has your interests at heart.

Just because a religious organization advertises on the radio or television doesn't mean it is legitimate. Implying that spiritual fulfillment can be purchased with money, many radio and television ministries utilize phony or irrelevant testimonials and falsely promise that donations will reap huge rewards and be used for a good cause. It is important to understand that more than two million people are ripped off each year by so-called religious groups that advertise on radio and television.

And remember, if you have been cheated by dishonest clergy or a phony ministry, first get mad and then get even; fight the culprits in court.

The Con Artists

"If I don't come up with $2000 they're going to kick my daughter out of college," Robert Riggio told Father Brady of Cody, Wyoming, during a late-night call. Father Brady wired Riggio $2000. "My mother got mugged last night and I don't have any money to help her out," Riggio told Father

Dalton of St. Richard's Catholic Church in Miami, Florida. Father Dalton wired the distressed caller $650. Using a wide variety of hard-luck stories, Riggio called Father Simmons of Ferry, Idaho, on at least 10 occasions. Father Simmons wired Riggio a total of $20,000 in 10 separate payments.

Posing as a parishioner with family problems, Robert Riggio, 44, persuaded 46 Catholic priests nationwide to wire him supposed loans ranging from $200 to $20,000. It took Riggio only 25 months and a dozen hard-luck stories to bilk the Catholic Church out of $133,606.

Using a creative collection of sad, sad stories, thousands of small-time con artists in the United States cheat churches, synagogues, mosques, and temples out of more than $70 million each year.

One of the most popular tactics used by these con artists is the "troubled traveler" or "stranded motorist" routine.

Sounding terrified, a woman who said her name was Pauline Taylor called William Massey at the First Baptist Church in Philadelphia and claimed to be one of his regular parishioners.

"Mrs. Taylor" explained that she was driving through a remote Maryland town with her two small children when her car developed transmission problems.

The hostile mechanic, Taylor told Massey, was refusing to let her leave the garage until she came up with $265 for the repairs, money she did not have. Massey could hear the scary sounding "mechanic" in the background making angry racial threats.

Within 10 minutes Massey had wired $265 to the troubled traveler. Massey was so concerned with the woman's safety he called the Maryland State Police and asked the troopers to try to find her.

Two days later, when the police located "Mrs. Taylor," they learned that she was a con artist using an assumed identity. The troopers arrested the woman along with her husband and 20-year-old sister.

Police in several states had been receiving reports from churches complaining that they had been bilked by phony parishioners with car problems.

When the police searched the hotel room where the three con artists had been staying, they discovered receipts for money that had been wired from churches in Washington, D.C., as well as New York, Pennsylvania, Maryland, Tennessee, Florida, Texas, and California.

The Nigerian Scam

More than 150 religious organizations have fallen victim to a version of the so-called Nigerian Scam. One church lost $102,000, three churches lost $90,000 or more, and another church lost $32,000. Dozens of religious groups have reported losing between $3000 and $30,000 to the Nigerian Scam.

Although the scenarios vary, the churches are typically contacted by someone who claims to be a prince, a businessman, or a high-ranking official from Nigeria who offers them the deal of a lifetime: "We would like to transfer $15 million from Lagos, Nigeria, to your account in the United States." Although the caller or writer is purposely vague about why this transfer is necessary, he usually explains that the procedure will exempt the money from Nigerian taxes or keep it out of the hands of corrupt officials.

"When the money is rerouted from your account back to Nigeria, it will be used to build churches and to spread God's word," several ministers were told.

"Naturally, we will compensate you for helping our endeavor," the so-called Nigerian VIP explains to his target. In most cases the ministers in the United States have been offered 20 percent of the $15 million to be transferred.

"Twenty percent of $15 million and the opportunity to help out a fellow Christian can be a very tempting proposition for many ministers—especially those who are naive about business," said an Indiana investigator who has researched several Nigerian scams.

At this point the Nigerian explains that before the $15 million can be sent, the minister will have to pay one to four percent of the $15 million for a service charge or perhaps to pay some sort of Nigerian tax.

"We already have most of the service charge," the Nigerian businessman told one minister, "so you only need to come up with $90,000."

After the minister sent the $90,000, the Nigerian contacted him again and explained that he needed another $7000 because he wanted to fly to the United States and deliver the $15 million personally.

Anxious to get his hands on 20 percent of $15 million, the minister borrowed another $7000 and wired it to Nigeria.

When the Nigerian businessman called a third time and regretfully explained, "The Nigerian government has increased the service charge rate—so you'll have to send an additional $22,000," the minister began to face up to the reality that he had been conned.

In 1994, St. Joseph's Cathedral in Sioux Falls, South Dakota, fell victim to a different version of the Nigeria-based scam.

Father Kettler, the parish priest, received a letter in November from the Senior Advocates Law Office in Lagos,

Nigeria, stating that a man named Harry Olson had left the cathedral $3 million in his will.

Hearing this good news, it's reasonable to assume that the church officials raised their hands to the heavens, gave thanks for the miracle, and, who knows, maybe even danced a bit of a jig. But there was one catch: The church was required to pay $90,000 in so-called taxes before it could pick up the $3 million. The church wired the money to Nigeria and Father Kettler made plans for a pilgrimage to Africa to pick up the church's windfall.

As Father Kettler got his tickets and passport in order, church officials heard that churches in Ohio, Texas, Missouri, and other states had received a similar letter.

It now became obvious that either the deceased Harry Olson was rich and religious enough to leave $3 million to a hundred different churches, or the entire affair was a hoax.

It was the latter. Church officials once again raised their hands to the heavens but this time it was to hit themselves on top of their heads.

Victimized by scores of scams in recent years, more than 4000 churches, synagogues, and other religious institutions have been forced to learn the old adage: "If it seems too good to be true, it probably is."

Protecting the Church's Money

Existing data strongly suggests that clerics—sensitive, good-natured, and well-intentioned—are frequently poorly informed about the tactics being used by white-collar criminals and con artists and are entirely too willing to subsidize crooks with parishioners' funds. One priest, accountable for a $3 million budget, was shocked to learn that a church secretary had pocketed $180,000 by inflating bills, using phantom employees, and paying for services that were never rendered. Although these tactics are as common as sin (and could have been thwarted if the church had required countersignatures on bill payments), the priest admitted, "Her tactics never even occurred to me."

The solution to this problem lies in education and the sharing of information. If information had been shared, 150 religious organizations would not have been suckered by the Nigerian Scam. Clerics aware of the stranded motorist con are more likely to check out stories and help the truly needy and less likely to line the pockets of criminals. One minister who was conned by the "sad, sad story" tactic gave $300 to an out-of-towner who had been "robbed of his wallet and credit cards." "If I had known that twelve other ministers had fallen for the same story, I would have asked the police to check the man out," said the minister.

In a sampling of 412 cases in which clerics were conned out of money, the criminals used the same six tactics over and over again. As with any enemy, if you are going to fight the devil, you had better learn his tactics.

Religious leaders should be aware that the devil wears many disguises. "She attended church almost every day," explained a priest who discovered that a 59-year-old bookkeeper had embezzled $88,000. A financial officer caught stealing from a synagogue was described as "deeply religious . . . a man totally devoted to Judaism." In a survey of 113 religious embezzlements (in which $7.9 million was stolen) 93 percent of the perpetrators were considered trusted, upstanding pillars of society by the church/synagogue leadership. Administrators and clergy who oversee parishioners' money must learn that embezzlers can be male or female, young or old, and are often articulate, well dressed, and personable. Denying this reality, too many leaders are failing to implement even basic financial controls and are allowing thieves to operate unchecked. Anyone can create an illusion of honesty, piety, and spirituality. Recognizing that everyone is potentially good or evil, guardians of God's purse need to rely more on audits and less on appearances.

Embezzling from the Church

Ellen F. Cooke, the former treasurer of the National Episcopal Church, led a life of unholy deception.

Her résumé stated that she had a degree in economics from Georgetown University. But Mrs. Cooke never attended Georgetown University, never earned a degree in economics, and, in fact, never graduated from any college. In reality, Mrs. Cooke attended George Washington University for two semesters, failed most of her courses, and then dropped out.

Creating a holier than thou image, Cooke told anyone who would listen that her wealthy Southern family had owned huge plantations, had lived in stately mansions, and had hidden their jewelry in draperies during the Civil War. "She gave the impression that she had grown up with servants and was used to socializing with royalty," said a female colleague who was laid off when the church suffered "unexplained budget problems."

In truth, Cooke's roots were mostly blue-collar, she did not inherit a fortune, and her family background was Catholic, not Episcopalian, as she led many to believe.

But her grandest deception was the illusion she created of being an honest, religious, and spiritual soul.

On May 1, 1995, the Episcopal Church's national office

in New York announced that the trusted treasurer had embezzled at least $2.2 million over five years from the church and its parishioners. Mrs. Cooke exploited her dual roles as treasurer and executive officer for administration and finance to steal from several church accounts.

Over the years, generous Episcopalians donated nearly 1000 trust funds and securities, worth more than $225 million, to their church. These donations accrued huge amounts of interest.

Believing that it is better to receive than to give, Mrs. Cooke transferred the interest on some of those funds to the church's operating account at the First American Bank in Washington, D.C., where she and her husband maintained personal accounts. No one was suspicious when the trusted treasurer would write checks made out to First American Bank to be transferred to another account at the same bank. After all, it was standard practice to move funds between various church accounts. But many of these checks were deposited in Cooke's personal accounts.

The *Washington Post* reported that in retrospect some of Cooke's colleagues did think it strange that she knew the account numbers of many trusts by heart.

Cooke stole $1.5 million from the bishops' discretionary funds (which are normally used for the homeless, widows facing eviction, and other people in need), wrote $225,000 in unauthorized checks to pay for jewelry, gifts, and her sons' private school, and charged $325,000 in personal expenses on her corporate credit card.

Her parishioners were less than ecstatic to learn that their 50-year-old treasurer, who was paid a generous $125,000-a-year salary, had embezzled $503,500 to purchase and renovate an 18th-century home in Montclair, New Jersey; $500,000 to purchase a 23-acre vacation farm in the Virginia countryside, complete with the heavenly smell of honeysuckle and the angelic sounds of a babbling brook; $16,000 for a Tiffany necklace; and hundreds of thousands more to pay for personal travel, clothes, fancy meals, extravagant gifts for friends and relatives, and other luxuries.

Mrs. Cooke's betrayal was particularly galling to the 100 loyal staff members she helped sack because of "diminished contributions and budget problems."

"Many people liked her," said a former employee who had a difficult time finding a new job, "but I always thought she was dictatorial, self-serving, and unqualified for such a high position."

Stung by more than $1 million in thefts from four churches, the Catholic Diocese of Cleveland, Ohio, set up surveillance cameras in 1987 and caught five trusted parishioners stealing from the collection plates. During 1989 in Minnesota, the wife of a Protestant pastor was convicted of stealing $100,000 from the church, where she served as a bookkeeper. And in 1990 in New City, New York, the treasurer of Christ Episcopal Church embezzled $267,000 and became a fugitive, leaving behind a wife and five children.

Ever since Judas Iscariot pilfered money that Jesus and his disciples set aside for the poor, people have been stealing from God's purse.

Preventing Embezzlement of Church Funds

If you suspect someone is stealing money from the church, blow the whistle! Embezzlers rarely operate in a vacuum; in most cases a friend, family member, coworker, or parishioner is very suspicious that something illegal is going on. In a sampling of 113 embezzlements from religious establishments, 68 perpetrators were caught because of whistleblowers. If you think you have evidence of financial shenanigans, report your suspicions to the proper authorities. It is important to catch thieves before they victimize others.

When financial discrepancies are discovered, act immediately; do not allow thieves to exploit statute of limitation laws. Dozens of embezzlers have gotten off scot-free and millions of dollars have been lost to churches and synagogues because audits were delayed and the suspected thefts were ignored. A man who stole $500,000 from a pension fund for Catholic priests could not be charged because of the statute of limitation. In that case, the priests lost $500,000 and the thief is living a life of luxury.

The Impersonation of Clergy

The impersonation of clergy has proven to be an extremely effective deceptive technique for a wide range of criminals.

During the last decade at least 945 criminals have posed as priests, rabbis, ministers, monks, and nuns in order to rob banks, scam religious establishments, and commit other crimes.

In Washington, D.C., a man known as "Father Crime" dressed as a priest and robbed at least 12 banks. Wearing a white collar, dark sunglasses, and a priest's black cassock and pants, the phony priest marched into banks, pulled out a handgun, and demanded money. After stuffing the generous contributions into a black bag, the husky, red-haired robber typically adjusted his white collar and casually walked from the bank.

Pretending to be a priest and a nun, a couple of con

artists in Prince George's County, Maryland, specialized in robbing older adults.

After obtaining relevant information about their targets by going through their mailboxes or by simply talking to neighbors, the criminal couple would knock at front doors and engage the homeowners in friendly conversation. "They knew my name and other things about me so I thought they were with my church or something," said a 79-year-old woman who was victimized.

Once the couple got invited into the home, the bogus priest would ask to use the bathroom while the phony nun engaged the victim in conversation. While the homeowner was distracted, the male con artist canvassed the house, stealing anything of value.

One elderly woman lost her entire life savings, which she had kept hidden in clothes in her closet. Unfortunately, the victim did not trust banks, but she did trust people who pretended to be priests and nuns.

Other victims lost thousands of dollars' worth of jewelry, credit cards, purses, cash, and other valuables.

In Vermont, a paroled white-collar criminal posed as a minister and became a one-man crime wave while conning an entire congregation.

Believing he was an ordained minister, four congregations in Vermont and Massachusetts welcomed John Weliczko with open arms.

But Weliczko was not a minister; he was a con artist on supervised release after being convicted of credit card, bank, and bankruptcy fraud in Massachusetts, Texas, and Illinois.

Before being caught and convicted in 1993 for impersonating a minister and violating his parole, Weliczko committed dozens of crimes in the name of God. In his role as minister, he befriended a dying woman in a hospital and then burglarized her home, stealing $10,000 worth of antiques and other valuables. After the woman died, he forged her name on her checks and stole an additional $4000.

The bogus pastor also collected money for illegally performed marriages, convinced an elderly parishioner to help him pay for his son's education (with a check made out to the pastor), and persuaded other church members to make him a beneficiary of their wills. When one woman allowed Weliczko to use her summer home, he stole and then sold her furniture.

Like all con artists who impersonate members of the clergy, Weliczko stole more than money from his parishioners; he stole their faith and shattered their trust.

During a time of grief or tragedy most people are comforted by having their priest, minister, or rabbi present. Capitalizing on any potential moneymaking venture, several con artists have dressed as clergy and exploited this tradition.

On January 16, 1982, bereaved relatives who huddled together in Washington, D.C., near the crash site of an Air Florida jetliner were comforted by the presence of a priest. They were also conned.

The man who claimed to be Rev. Michael Ryan was actually escaped convict William W. Emlinger. Emlinger, who had a history of showing up at disaster scenes, specialized in gaining the confidence of relatives and later burglarizing their homes.

Emlinger was inadvertently caught by ABC News' *Nightline.* Law enforcement officials who were watching the news program immediately recognized Emlinger as an escaped prisoner, even though he was wearing a clerical collar, and took him into custody.

The Real Thing

In many cases, legitimate clergy have turned out to be impostors. About 60 priests, rabbis, and ministers each year are caught embellishing their résumés and lying about their backgrounds.

On August 7, 1990, in Fort Lewis, Washington, the U.S. Army court-martialed and fined Major Gary Probst, a 37-year-old Mormon minister, for lying about his military record and wearing combat medals he had not earned.

Authorities discovered that the career chaplain was actually a student at Brigham Young University in Utah at the time he claimed to be a soldier in Vietnam.

"Just what we all need," said a Special Forces sergeant familiar with the case, "a chaplain who is a fraud."

Major Probst never served in Vietnam as he claimed and was never awarded the six medals, including the Bronze Star for bravery, he so proudly wore on his chest. "I wonder what else he lied about?" the sergeant continued.

In Salt Lake City, during 1991, another Mormon Church elder got caught embellishing his past. This time the church leader pretended to be both a war hero and a professional baseball player. Both stories were lies.

After being caught in the lies, Paul H. Dunn, a popular inspirational writer and member of the church's hierarchy, apologized publicly for the fraud. "I confess that I have not always been accurate in my public talks and writings," he said in a open letter to the church. "Furthermore, I have indulged in other activities inconsistent with the high and sacred office which I have held."

"The bottom line," complained a longtime member of the Mormon religion, "is that he used lies to help his career so he could make more money."

Dunn made up stories about buddies dying in his arms in World War II and falsely claimed to have played baseball for the St. Louis Cardinals.

"I don't know which is worse," said a detective who has arrested six clergy impersonators and four legitimate priests and rabbis during his 22-year law enforcement career, "a crook who pretends to be a member of the clergy or a member of the clergy who is a crook."

Identifying False Clergy

Be aware of impostors. Just as shiny lures attract hungry trout, well-funded religious organizations are notorious for attracting unqualified and dishonest impostors to handle their money.

When a group of ministers in Maryland hired David Robinson to manage finances and handle legal issues, they thought they had the perfect man for the job. But that was before Robinson was charged with stealing $700,000. Robinson did not have the academic credentials he listed on his résumé; did not have a law degree as he claimed; and was, in fact, a convicted felon who had defrauded businesses of $70,000.

Robinson was just one of hundreds of unqualified and dishonest impostors who have been hired by churches and synagogues in recent years.

Be wary if a clergy member asks for a large sum of money. Don't sign over power of attorney—even to your priest—unless you're certain he's on the up-and-up. If you give your minister the power to pay your bills, be very specific as to which bills will be paid and put a limit on how much money can be spent each month. Just because someone has the title of minister, priest, or rabbi doesn't guarantee that that person has your best interests at heart.

Tips for Fighting Back

- Face up to the facts. Many religious groups sound like legitimate institutions of worship but are actually corrupt. Be careful—they might only be out to take your money. Individuals who believe that all church organizations are good and that all clergy members are honest are more likely to be financially victimized.

- Parishioners need to be cautious and question motives if they are considering allowing clergy to invest their money, pay their bills, take control of their checkbooks, take over power of attorney, or control their estate.

- If you have been cheated by dishonest clergy or a phony minister, fight the culprits in court.

- When a clergy member has been bilked out of church money, it is important to share that information so that other churches are not similarly victimized. In a sampling of 412 cases in which clerics were conned out of money, the criminals used the same six tactics over and over again.

- Religious leaders should be aware that embezzlers can often be hard to spot. Anyone can give the impression of being honest, religious, and spiritual. Guardians of God's purse need to rely more on audits and less on appearances.

- Be aware of impostors. Religious organizations are notorious for attracting unqualified and dishonest impostors to handle their money.

- If you suspect someone is stealing money from the church, blow the whistle! It is important to catch thieves before they victimize others.

- When financial discrepancies are discovered, act immediately; do not allow thieves to exploit statute of limitation laws.

C H A P T E R 7

The Banking Mess

If the savings and loan (S&L) disaster of the 1980s taught the public one thing, it's that nobody can rob a bank like a banker. Nobody!

Financial Disasters and Rogue Traders

The Savings and Loan Crisis

Hitting like a nuclear explosion, the S&L crisis continues to result in economic fallout worldwide and has cost the American taxpayer $500 billion—more than the Vietnam War—a sum that translates into a $2000 loss for every man, woman, and child in the United States. The attack left 1000 thrifts dead and every U.S. citizen wounded.

Although it's often difficult to determine where mismanagement and gross negligence end and thievery begins, at least 40 percent of the $500-billion S&L crisis was the direct result of white-collar crime—embezzlement, fraud, and other financial shenanigans. Without the crime there wouldn't have been a crisis.

A national symbol of greed and arrogance, Charles H. Keating Jr., former owner of the Lincoln Savings and Loan Association, was convicted of looting his bank and defrauding investors of more than $250 million. Lincoln Savings' failure cost taxpayers $2.6 billion, with $962 million of that loss directly attributed to Keating's wrongdoing.

Giving new meaning to the word nepotism, Lincoln's parent company, American Continental Corporation (ACC), included Keating's son, daughter, and son-in-law among its top officers. These family members, ages 24 to 28, received salaries of up to $900,000. Incredibly, from 1985 to 1988 Keating and his family received $34 million in salaries and other benefits from ACC.

Sadly, Keating was only one of hundreds of bankers who contributed to the S&L crisis.

On May 27, 1986, Jeffrey A. Levitt, owner of Maryland's Old Court Savings and Loan Association, pleaded guilty to 25 counts of embezzling and misappropriating $14.6 million of his depositors' money. He was sentenced to 30 years in prison for his crimes but was paroled seven years later.

Levitt, who was an inner-city landlord before becoming Old Court's CEO, was once convicted of 500 housing-code violations, and was even shot in the buttocks by an irate tenant who couldn't get his plumbing fixed. Although he was allowed to run a thrift institution with more than $800 million in assets, Levitt had also been threatened with disbarment and was suspended from practicing law after lying to a judge about his ownership of a rental property.

Adding salt to the taxpayers' wounds, scores of convicted S&L executives have received slap-on-the-wrist sentences, have been released from prison after serving only a fraction of their terms, and have been allowed to default on their plea-bargained assurances that they would pay fines and restitution in order to avoid longer prison terms.

In 2610 court cases, judges ordered S&L crooks to pay approximately $900 million in fines and restitution. To date, less than four percent of this money has been recovered.

Still reeling from the S&L crisis, the world's banking industry and, therefore, the world's economy would soon be rocked by three new scandals: the collapse of the Bank of Credit and Commerce International (BCCI); the bankruptcy of Barings PLC, one of Britain's oldest investment banks; and the announcement of an attempted cover-up of $1.1 billion in losses at Daiwa Bank's New York office.

The Bank of Credit and Commerce International

In 1991, after discovering that $20 billion had been lost or stolen from the Bank of Credit and Commerce International—now more commonly referred to as the Bank of Crooks and Criminals International—and that thousands of people had lost their entire savings, regulators from 62 countries marched in and shut BCCI down.

In what is considered one of the largest bank frauds in world financial history, BCCI was found to be a massive criminal enterprise that laundered drug money, sold weapons on the black market, and helped dictators like Manuel Noriega, Saddam Hussein, and Ferdinand Marcos embezzle from their national treasuries.

Utilizing such business practices as bribery, extortion, and kidnappings, BCCI became the bank of choice for underworld mobsters and international terrorists such as Abu Nidal.

On October 19, 1994, a federal judge sentenced Swaleh Naqvi, the former chief executive of BCCI, to eight years in prison and ordered him to pay $255.4 million in restitution.

In handing down the sentence, Judge Joyce Hens Green said that the fraud represented a grave threat to the United States banking system, which could have been weakened by the bank's huge concealed debt.

"Without your leadership, without your continuing criminal activity, the loss would not have been as large," Judge Green said from the bench.

No one connected with the case, or familiar with the U.S. criminal justice system, expects that Naqvi, 61, will ever pay the restitution.

The Collapse of Barings

Barings PLC, one of Britain's most prestigious banking houses, was founded in 1762. It went bankrupt February 26, 1995, after a lone 28-year-old British trader named Nick Leeson lost about $1.4 billion by gambling the bank's money, apparently without authorization or supervision, on high-risk Asian derivatives.

Leeson, who was based in Singapore, attempted to go on the lam but was arrested March 2, 1995, when he got off a plane in Frankfurt, Germany.

"We still have many unanswered questions concerning Leeson," said a British investigator who is intimately involved with the case. "But I guarantee that this fiasco is largely due to criminal and illegal behavior and that the economic reverberations will soon hit the United States."

On December 2, 1995, a judge in Singapore said that Leeson "spun a web of deceit" that was "deliberately designed to beguile" and sentenced him to 6½ years in prison.

The Daiwa Bank Scandal

Toshihide Iguchi, the 44-year-old central figure in the spectacular bond-trading scandal at Daiwa Bank in New York, pleaded guilty on October 20, 1995, to hiding $1.1 billion in losses over a 12-year period. Iguchi, the baby-faced head of U.S.-government-bond trading at Daiwa Bank's Manhattan office, had made an astronomical 30,000 unauthorized transactions while trying to cover up the losses.

The Fall of Paul: Corrupt Bankers

David L. Paul, the former CenTrust chairman who once ruled an $11-billion banking empire out of Miami, was used to the good life.

Sunning himself aboard his 40-foot sailboat, *Bodacious*, or his $7-million, 94-foot yacht, *Grand Cru*, where he stashed $50,000 in petty cash, Paul sipped aged wine from Baccarat crystal goblets, flicked ashes from Cuban cigars into Tiffany ashtrays, and basked in his own importance.

Paul hobnobbed with the rich and famous, conducted telephone conversations from the back of his chauffeur-driven Mercedes stretch limo, and traveled the world in his private jet.

Insisting on the finest of accommodations, Paul enjoyed a multimillion-dollar mansion on the Miami waterfront and a heavenly home in Connecticut and once ran up a $45,000 hotel tab during a short stay in New York. His meals were usually prepared by personal chefs, and he ate from Limoges china.

Known for his gigantic galas that cost his depositors as much as $122,000, Paul, like a modern-day Gatsby, hosted celebrities such as Elizabeth Taylor and turned parties into events. For one social gathering he flew six chefs in from France.

Paul's penthouse office suite atop the I. M. Pei–designed CenTrust Towers was decorated—at depositors' expense—with a $30-million collection of old masters, including works by Flemish artist Peter Paul Rubens, and had a private bathroom adorned with gold-plated fixtures. Visitors to the sky lobby sipped coffee served on silver trays and strolled soulfully past some of the finest sculpture ever displayed in a bank office building.

The personification of greed and arrogance, Paul paid himself a total of $16 million—$66,000 per week—during his tour as chairman and looked down on his depositors from atop a gleaming skyscraper, an opulent symbol of excess, 47 stories above the city.

On Monday, January 2, 1995, at 12:50 P.M., Paul, 55, checked into the Federal Correctional Institution in Tallahassee to start serving an 11-year term for racketeering and bank and securities fraud.

As the former high-powered executive stepped through the gates he was stripped of his possessions, handed a prison uniform, and issued a new name—Prisoner No. 37935-004.

In addition to his 11-year prison sentence, which many argue was much too light, Paul was ordered to pay $65 million for his part in the 1991 collapse of CenTrust. The failure cost U.S. taxpayers a whopping $1.7 billion.

Paul was convicted of stealing $3.1 million in bank funds for his personal use, and the crimes he committed while at CenTrust caused the bank and the taxpayers to lose an additional $380 million.

During a long and expensive trial—which took more money from taxpayers—the public learned that Paul hurt thousands of innocent people and arrogantly broke any law that stood in the way of his greed and personal ambitions.

The big-shot banker was exposed as a crook and an impostor.

Paul had long boasted in his official CenTrust biography, and swore under oath in court, that he had a Ph.D. from Harvard and an M.B.A. from Columbia. But he was lying. Confronted with the truth, Paul conceded to the jury that he had manufactured the Harvard and Columbia degrees and confessed that he had lied under oath about the degrees in previous court cases.

Protecting Yourself—Where We Went Wrong

Using such tools as scissors and paste, both Leeson and Iguchi produced laughably flagrant forgeries to keep their scams going. Iguchi hid his activities by falsifying account statements, and Leeson cut up routine financial documents and pasted them together to produce fake bank statements.

But why were their managers so out of the loop that these scams could be perpetuated? As shining stars, both Leeson and Iguchi developed super-trader mystiques that either blinded financial managers or caused them to look the other way. Supervisors are loath to question or to stand in the way of moneymaking machines.

Paul, on the other hand, was able to steal an embarrassment of riches for himself by embracing so fully the spectacle of greed. But why did it take him so long to get caught?

In each case, proper auditing procedures would have caught the deceptions before they snowballed out of control.

It also appears that both Barings and Daiwa Bank violated a cardinal rule of thumb aimed at protecting society from employees who can move tens of millions of dollars in a single trade: Keep the trading and auditing responsibilities separate. Since Leeson and Iguchi were both responsible for overseeing the documentary settlement of their own trades, both lacked supervision and both were essentially reporting to themselves.

As with all banking fraud, the S&L crisis and the scandals at BCCI, Barings PLC, and Daiwa Bank could and should have been prevented.

The tragic flaw—the common theme that runs through all of these banking scandals—is that too much power and authority were given to one person while standard checks and balances were ignored.

Fraud and embezzlement in the banking industry is absolutely preventable.

Bankers are fond of saying, "Fraud is the price of doing business." But it is important to understand that this "price" will be paid by the customers, not the bankers.

Electronic Banking

The events that occurred from June to October 1994 were an $11.6-million lesson in the risks of electronic banking.

Using a personal computer and passwords that may have been provided by bank insiders, Vladimir Leonidovich

Levin, a 34-year-old computer expert, tapped into Citibank's central computer in New York from his office in St. Petersburg, Russia, and illegally transferred $11.6 million into accounts opened by accomplices at banks in California and Israel.

Authorities have arrested Levin and six other people involved in the case and have recovered all but $400,000 of the $11.6 million, but the incident sounded a message, loud and clear, to the world's banking establishment: Computer hackers are capable of stealing millions, even billions of dollars from banks.

As dozens of cases have illustrated, banks are especially vulnerable to illegal electronic transfer schemes and wire fraud when a bank employee is either assisting with the transfer or providing valuable inside information.

In 1991, Mildred M. Young, 43, who supervised wire transfers of money at the now-defunct Madison National Bank in Washington, D.C., pleaded guilty to embezzling $423,172 from the bank over a five-year period.

Using the special access her position provided, Young electronically diverted other people's money from Madison National Bank, where she was employed, to her personal account at Sovran Bank.

The 34 separate acts of wire fraud were never noticed until Madison collapsed and outside auditors began poring over the books.

Madison's failure cost the U.S. bank insurance fund approximately $160 million.

"The really scary part of all this," said a computer-security expert with a bank in Washington, D.C., "is that there are many ways a bank can be robbed electronically . . . and it's sometimes done by unsophisticated amateurs."

On August 24, 1995, in Columbus, Ohio, Rev. John T. Coats II, 27, a member of the staff at the Centenary United Methodist Church and the former vice president of the Columbus NAACP chapter, was sentenced to six months in prison and home confinement for stealing $78,825 from National City Bank.

Coats and two coconspirators, Michelle Nelson, 34, and James M. Gray III, 40, used false names and identification to open up a series of accounts in 10 banks. Possibly benefiting from inside help, the three bank robbers were able to obtain the identification number of a bank employee. Pretending to be that employee, the trio telephoned National City Bank headquarters and requested that various amounts of money be transferred into the bogus accounts.

The two men and one woman then marched into the 10 separate banks, politely handed the tellers withdrawal slips, and pranced out with fists full of cash.

Most banks proudly proclaim that their computerized accounts are secured with secret passwords and identification numbers. But most banks also suffer security leaks and have at least one employee who is willing to sell so-called secret information to the highest bidder.

Computer hacker Justin Tanner Peterson, 34, who calls himself "Agent Steal," admitted on August 29, 1994, that he conspired to transfer $150,000 from a branch of Heller Financial Inc., in Glendale, California, to the Union Bank account of a coconspirator.

He also pleaded guilty to possessing 40 secret computer passwords from accounts at TRW, Heller Financial, and America Online.

To cover up the theft, Peterson and his coconspirators telephoned phony bomb threats to the bank so that the employees would be evacuating the building at the time the money was being transferred.

Peterson gained national notoriety when he and another well-known hacker, Kevin Poulsen, rigged telephone lines at three radio stations that were conducting contests and offering valuable prizes. By rigging the lines, Peterson and Poulsen also rigged the contests and won two trips to Hawaii, two Porsches, and prize money totaling $50,000.

Bit by bit, case by case, computer-age Bonnie and Clydes are learning how to rob banks without firing a shot or depending on a getaway driver. Many of the attempted robberies have failed, but with each attempt the crooks get closer to breaking the codes and breaking the bank. They are learning from their mistakes.

On February 10, 1993, in New Jersey, the FBI arrested five low-level mafia members from New York and charged them with conspiracy to divert nearly $50 million by wire transfer from Bankers Trust Co. in New York to an account in Philadelphia.

The scheme unraveled because a cooperating witness provided the FBI with advance notice of the plot.

Although the five arrested thugs, whose average age was 54, were not exactly computer-literate, they did manage to gain access to wire-transfer accounts, they obtained the proper bank coding, and they had the connections to discover that a wire transfer of $49,854,292 had been sent from a bank in Chicago to Bankers Trust Co. in New York.

And while they were certainly amateurs at transferring money, the group did show a certain tenacity and a willingness to learn from past mistakes; this was the third money transfer scheme they had attempted.

They bungled a chance to transfer $5 million in October 1992 for the most banal of reasons, when one of the members transposed two digits in an account number, canceling the transaction. The group successfully transferred $25 million in January 1993, but had the transfer negated because an account name had been listed incorrectly in the accompanying transfer documents.

Electronic embezzlement, "the crime of the future," has actually been around for many, many years.

On May 13, 1988, in Chicago, another gang of men including Gabriel Taylor, 27, an $18,000-a-year wire-transfer clerk at First National Bank of Chicago, and Armand Moore, a burly 33-year-old ex-con, came very close—much closer than the banking industry cares to admit—to stealing $68.7 million.

Moore, who liked to refer to himself as "the Chairman," was paroled from prison in 1986 after serving only four years of an 11-year sentence for bank fraud. He had been jailed for creating a fake bank (actually a telephone answering service) and issuing himself letters of credit. The documents were so realistic that 10 air-charter companies leased planes to Moore so he could jet cross-country in style like a Fortune 500 executive. When Moore was finally caught he owed $180,000, which, it's safe to assume, he didn't pay.

Rehabilitation being what it is, Moore began planning his next caper shortly after his early release from prison. Hearing from his cousin that a guy named Gabriel Taylor was working at First National, Moore suggested that he and the bank employee have a little chat.

Apparently charmed by the Chairman, Taylor decided to go along with his proposed plan for a $28 million portion of the take.

At 8:30 A.M. on Friday the 13th, one of Moore's accomplices pretended to be a Merrill Lynch executive and called First National to arrange for the electronic transfer of $24 million from Merrill Lynch's account to an account the gang had set up in Vienna's Creditanstalt bank. When the impostor heard the recorded message, "This is First National Bank of Chicago, your call is being taped," he told one of Taylor's unwitting coworkers to send the money. While this was occurring, Taylor pretended to telephone another Merrill Lynch official for a backup confirmation. He actually called another gang member who could later be heard giving an official-sounding "Approved" on the tape of the transaction. A few keystrokes and a few seconds later the $24 million was wired to New York's Citibank for later transfer to Vienna.

Another call, purportedly from Brown-Forman, makers of Jack Daniels whiskey, arrived at First National 30 minutes later. The gang followed the same routine. A gang member, pretending to be a Brown-Forman executive and using the correct code words for the Brown-Forman account, ordered $19.7 million sent directly to the account set up in Vienna. A code and a password were entered into the computer and *zap*, $19.7 million arrived in the gang's account in Vienna.

Thirty minutes later a third call arrived, this time from an impostor pretending to be an executive with United Airlines. *Zap*, and $25 million sailed smooth as silk from the United account to Citibank for relay to the gang's account in Vienna.

On Monday, May 16, 1988, as the gang sat around smoking big cigars and dreaming of faraway places, the scheme broke down.

After the funds were transferred, Merrill Lynch and United did not have enough money in their accounts to cover outstanding checks, which had already started to bounce. The more the bankers at First National looked into the problem the more they realized that something was amiss.

Although the exact turn of events at this point is unknown, it is easy to visualize a top executive at First National screaming, "Oh my god!—Somebody call the FBI!"

After a little chat with the FBI, Taylor decided to name his coconspirators and agreed to make incriminating phone calls to his accomplices, which the FBI taped as evidence.

In the meantime, First National was able to retrieve the funds sent to Vienna and halted the transfers from Citibank. The entire $68.7 million was returned.

As the would-be millionaires sit in jail, they are certainly haunted by a few essential what-ifs.

What if there had been more money in the accounts? What if the conspirators had settled for a mere $20 million? What if they had selected an account that was less active?

Except for a few minor flaws in their plan, the gang might very well be sunning themselves in a far-off place and smoking big cigars.

Preventing Electronic Theft

Banks have got to make a better effort to guard confidential customer information.

In 1992, a thief stole credit reports at the credit union on Capitol Hill that serves House of Representatives employees and used the confidential information to obtain fraudulent loans and credit cards. In thousands of other recorded cases, thieves have used information obtained from computers, from bank trash bins, and from unwitting or dishonest bank employees to steal billions of dollars. Information needs to be guarded like cash. Bank directors need to ask, "How might this information be stolen and utilized by crooks?" and then implement procedures to guard against leaks.

Who has access to computerized information? How much confidential information is lying around on unguarded desks? Can passersby read what is on an office computer screen? How vulnerable is the mail? How much information can be provided to telephone callers? Is the caller an impostor? Does the caller have a need for or a right to this information? Have employees been briefed about not discussing VIP accounts with friends, family, and other outsiders? (This is a huge problem.) Do employees know the consequences and penalties of such behavior? How easy would it be for an outside computer hacker to obtain private information?

If banks could prevent leaks of personal financial information, they would prevent over $500 million in fraud each year.

Automatic Teller Machines

While Karen Smith was cheering and screaming at a high school football game in Gresham, Oregon, on November 18, 1994, thieves were breaking into her van in the parking lot.

According to police, the thieves, two men and a woman, stole her automatic teller machine (ATM) card and discovered a crook's gold mine in the process: Ms. Smith had jotted down her personal identification number (PIN) on her Social Security card.

"Yeeeehaaa!" the crooks must have hollered. "We're going to have a high ole time this weekend!"

But at that point the crooks had no idea that they had hit the mother lode.

Karen Smith didn't find out what a good time the thieves had and didn't even know her card was missing until her credit union called to tell her that her account was $346,770 overdrawn.

"What!" she probably responded.

"Since Friday night someone has used your ATM card to withdraw $346,770 from 48 bank machines," she was told.

"What!"

The thieves had probably never worked so hard in their lives or with more enthusiasm.

Authorities reported that, traveling more than 100 miles through five counties, the trio used Ms. Smith's ATM card to make 724 withdrawals in 54 hours. For the thieves it was like winning the lottery—again and again and again.

To safeguard against such theft, most ATMs are programmed to give no more than $200 or $300 a day on any single card. But because of a computer-program change at the Oregon TelCo Credit Union, the system was out of whack that weekend.

When the computer showed that Ms. Smith's account was empty, the crooks reportedly repeatedly fed empty bank envelopes into the automated tellers and punched in bogus deposits until Ms. Smith's balance read $820,500.

In this case, the machine believed that the card users were actually depositing the money and posted the new balance right away.

Police immediately suspected that David Gallagher, who

had been in prison five times, and his wife Terry, both 40, might be involved in the caper.

Putting the two under surveillance, the police noticed that they had purchased a new pickup truck, and acquaintances reported that the couple claimed to have won a $50,000 jackpot in Reno. Terry Gallagher, the investigators learned, was telling friends she was about to inherit $500,000 from a relative.

Security cameras at several of the ATMs showed that there were three people using Ms. Smith's card and that the perpetrators were driving a maroon Cadillac. The owner of the Cadillac, police believed, was Danny Ballow, 47.

Convinced that they had the culprits, police obtained search warrants, found $30,000 in the suspects' home, and arrested Danny Ballow and the Gallaghers.

The suspects face 63-year prison terms. And who knows, maybe David Gallagher, who has 21 felony convictions, will finally be prevented from victimizing society.

Although some media reports stated that the $346,770 theft was the largest ever from an automatic teller machine, in truth it was only the sixth largest theft involving an ATM. Hundreds of white-collar criminals have stolen amounts ranging from $10,000 to $100,000.

Some bandits use binoculars to observe PINs being used by customers. The crooks then match the PINs up with the account numbers on discarded transaction slips. One woman reportedly purchased a new home with funds she stole using that tactic.

Several crooks have stocked ATMs with rigged, phony deposit slips that directed other customers' money into their accounts.

At least a dozen enterprising thieves have used forklifts and other heavy equipment or just brute strength to cart away entire machines. While most of these crooks have stolen machines packed with money, some have carried the ATMs away, sawed them open, and risked years in prison for what turned out to be an empty machine.

A 35-year-old Polish-born electronics expert and former ATM repairman didn't steal the machines, but he did obtain something almost as valuable. By peering over customers' shoulders and retrieving their trashed banking receipts, he obtained the PINs and the bank-account numbers needed to activate the computerized tellers. Using his encoding machine, he then added strips of magnetic tape, bearing the stolen digital codes, to his plastic cards and used the counterfeit ATM cards to steal $86,000.

On May 13, 1993, in Hartford, Connecticut, federal investigators announced that they were searching for three clean-cut men with banking and computer expertise who had staged a unique, high-tech bank robbery.

The three men rolled their own ATM into the Buckland Hills Mall on April 24, 1993, and then sabotaged the other mall ATMs so that customers would be forced to use theirs.

More than 3000 people attempted to use the ATM during the next two weeks, but none were able to retrieve any money. However, the machine did record the 3000 bank accounts and personal identification numbers of the unsuspecting customers.

The three perpetrators then used the purloined information to encode their own blank cards and withdrew over $63,000 from scores of accounts.

Insulating Yourself from ATM Theft

Automatic Teller Machine cards, or ATM cards, are increasingly being exploited by crooks, but there's a lot you can do to protect yourself.

Here are some simple ways to start: Do not leave your card in a place that is easily accessible for thieves. Memorize your personal identification number (PIN); do not write the number down and leave it where a thief can find it. When using the ATM, don't let those in line behind you see you enter your PIN. Be aware of the schemes con artists have used to obtain PIN numbers.

Remember that after stealing purses, many criminals will telephone the victim and pretend to be either the police or a bank official. "We have caught the man who stole your purse," the impostor will say. "We need your PIN number to determine if he has stolen any money from your account."

Finally, it's important to check all ATM transactions on your monthly bank statements and report any inconsistencies immediately.

Credit Card Fraud

Banks, lawmakers, and individual card owners need to do more to help prevent credit card fraud. In 1994, banks issuing Visa and MasterCards lost more than $700 million to fraud artists. When losses of department stores, oil companies, and other credit cards are combined with the losses of Visa and MasterCards, the total losses are nearly $3 billion a year. Approximately 580,000 Visa and MasterCard accounts were affected by fraud in 1994. Although many consumers are told that the losses are absorbed by the system, nothing could be further from the truth.

Ultimately, the losses translate into higher interest and finance charges and get worked back into the cost of banking and other services. Fraud can also affect the credit ratings of honest card holders, fouling up loan applications and causing other problems for years to come. Consequently, it is the honest card owner who eventually pays for the losses created by criminals. The most effective weapon against credit card fraud is education. The more that bankers, lawmakers, and card owners know about fraud operations the better they will be at countering those operations.

What Banks Can Do

To begin with, banks should stop throwing customer credit card numbers and other private financial information in the trash. In Atlanta, Georgia, 30 people were charged with a $10-million bank fraud scheme. The Dumpster-diving defendants, who defrauded people in 17 states, used checks, credit card receipts, bank statements, and other documents found in trash bins to produce counterfeit checks, phony driver's licenses, and false credit cards.

Employees should be thoroughly briefed on the importance of confidentiality of customer records; anyone abusing this information for criminal purposes should be prosecuted. It is a good idea to treat blank cards as cash, locking them up in a safe, protected area. Conduct in-depth background investigations into key personnel to assure that you are hiring honest people of good character who haven't committed crimes in the past. Learn the many tactics being used in job application fraud and implement procedures to guard against it.

Banks must also beware of credit card application fraud. Practitioners obtain a cardholder's information and then send in an entirely new application in the customer's name but at a different address. This way, the criminal gets credit cards the legitimate holder doesn't even know about. In some cases the criminals make the minimum monthly payment for a few months so they can keep running up the tab. After obtaining customer information, some crooks will call a bank and state, "My credit card has been lost—would you please send me a new card to my *new* address?" It would be a small matter for a bank to contact the cardholder and inquire whether he or she requested that a new card be sent to a new address.

A new service called the Issuers Clearinghouse Service is designed to catch application fraud by checking all new applications against existing accounts and against a list of known telephone numbers, mail drops, and dead Social Security numbers that have been used in past frauds. If the system shows that there are 20 new applications from a single post office box, issuers are warned that something is fishy.

New technology and procedures such as Fraud Early Warning System, used by Visa and others, can help head off many scams. Although controversial from a privacy point of view, computer profiles that analyze customers' spending can alert security personnel if uncharacteristic charges are suddenly being made. These profiles have prevented a lot of fraud. The profile of one cardholder showed that he never charged anything over $75, always used his card in the same city at the same six stores, and usually purchased items such as jeans, work clothes, and groceries. When his card was suddenly being used at several Victoria's Secret shops and to charge expensive jewelry and meals in three different cities, the computer "red flagged" the purchases and put an end to a costly fraud. Visa and other companies are now encoding extra digits in the magnetic stripe of its cards. These digits don't show on the account number but are required in the electronic verification process. Since these secret digits are present only on legitimate cards, it is easy to spot counterfeits.

Many credit card issuers now require recipients of new or replacement cards to call a certain telephone number to activate them. Utilizing a caller ID system, banks check the activation call against the cardholder's home and work numbers. If they don't match, the call is kicked over to a bank employee who will make additional inquiries.

What Lawmakers Can Do

Many laws and regulations—including too-lenient bankruptcy laws—are helping the criminals and harming individuals.

On December 1, 1995, in California, more than 20 people, mostly Vietnamese immigrants, were arrested in a vast credit card scam that bilked banks and stores out of $100 million nationwide. Taking advantage of federal consumer credit regulations, the immigrants would temporarily increase their credit card limits by sending banks checks for much more than they owed—so-called booster checks—even though they knew the checks would bounce. Since banks are required to credit accounts the day a check arrives (before a bad check has time to bounce) the cardholders ran up expensive purchases and took out cash advances.

When the banks came looking for the cardholders, the

fraud artists took advantage of another legal loophole so frequently utilized by white-collar criminals: they simply declared bankruptcy. One woman, a city employee, ran up a credit card debt of $615,000 even though she took home only $1000 per month from her job. Regulations that create a window of opportunity for fraud are being exploited by a wide range of white-collar criminals including doctors, teachers, and lawyers.

In Dade County, Florida, a judge who had just pleaded guilty to corruption went out and charged $100,000 in luxuries on a dozen different credit cards. He then filed for bankruptcy and avoided paying even a single penny back to his creditors.

It's time that we changed the laws and regulations that are helping the crooks and hurting the honest consumer.

Protecting Yourself from Credit Card Fraud

To avoid being a victim of fraud, a consumer needs to watch his or her credit cards with an eagle eye, keep track of receipts, and scrutinize the monthly statements. If you see a suspicious charge, call the 800 number on the statement and ask for an explanation. The next step is to put your complaint in writing. Do so within 30 days or you could be liable for the fraudulent charges. In most cases, the consumer is liable for only $50 if his or her credit card is lost, stolen, or used by an unauthorized person.

Never give out a credit card number over the phone to an unknown party, such as an unsolicited caller offering to sell something or saying you've won a prize. And if you use a cellular phone to relay your numbers to a legitimate party, unauthorized scanners can pick them up.

Do not give out your Social Security number, your date

of birth, or your mother's maiden name unless you know whom you are dealing with and have assurance that the information will be held in the strictest confidence.

Take all receipts and either file or destroy them. Tear up the carbon charge slip because it contains your card numbers.

Don't put your credit card number on the Internet. Issuers are trying to find a secure way to execute credit card transactions on the Net but the kinks haven't been worked out yet.

If your card is missing, immediately call the company that issued it.

Don't write your credit card number on the outside of envelopes, and don't sign blank charge slips.

Don't leave your wallet or purse in your vehicle. This is especially important if you are jogging, hiking, golfing, or using a health club; thieves are increasingly targeting parked vehicles at these locations. If you have to keep your wallet or purse in the car, hide them beneath objects in the trunk. Try not to be too conspicuous that you are putting your cards in the trunk; thieves watch to see where drivers place their valuables.

Remember to be street smart. Be aware of the devious and creative ways crooks have obtained credit cards. Bar workers sometimes jam credit cards out of sight into the pockets of leather books used to deliver bills to the table. Customers, especially drunk ones, often sign, leave, and forget the card. During September 1995, a nurse at the Maryland Shock Trauma Center stole credit cards from a police officer who was undergoing surgery for three bullet wounds. The nurse charged $15,000 on the officer's credit cards. In California, an employee of the Los Angeles County coroner pleaded guilty to using credit cards belonging to dead people. And in Florida, a 35-year-old professional caregiver was convicted of using the credit cards belonging to her frail, elderly clients.

When you're traveling, ask for the carbons of car rental agreements and destroy them. Don't leave the rental agreement in the car, because it includes a driver's license number, account number, and address. Shred travel itineraries and ticket receipts issued by airlines and travel agents. Don't be conned into writing your address, Social Security number, or telephone number on credit card slips. Don't write your credit card account number on checks. Don't let a clerk write your driver's license number on your check if it's the same as your Social Security number.

Credit card thieves are increasingly focusing their attention on your mailbox. It is best to have your mail delivered through the slot in your front door. Unprotected curbside mailboxes are extremely vulnerable. Communal mail rooms in apartment buildings should have strong locks on each occupant's mailbox, not the type of lock that can be picked with a butter knife. Destroy all preapproved credit card applications before discarding. If your monthly statement doesn't arrive on time, call the issuer immediately. After delivery, empty your mail receptacle as soon as possible. Report any suspicious activity to the police or the U.S. Postal Service. Rewards are sometimes paid by the U.S. Postal Service for information that leads to a conviction for mail theft.

Don't be misled by deceptive credit card solicitations. In 1994, Credicorp Inc. was fined $4 million after it was determined the company misled consumers. Credicorp mailed offers of a "Gold Card" with a $10,000 line of credit that required customers to pay $29.95. Consumers who paid the fee received a credit card that could be used only for merchandise offered by the company through its catalog. Another company offering gold cards instructed applicants to call a 976 telephone number, which automatically put a $49.95 charge on the consumer's telephone bill as a one-time card membership fee. Only after making the call did consumers learn that there was an additional $30 fee for the card, which could be used only to purchase items from catalogs.

Why does your credit card charge interest rates of 18 to 21 percent? Why do you and people with bad credit continue to receive unsolicited preapproved applications for credit cards? Because the banks and credit card issuers want you to pay for the credit card fraud and bad credit decisions that they make. Credit card fraud is largely the result of the issuers' being willing to give up control and to accept bad debt and forgeries. They are willing to accept this because their earnings and profit (theirs, not yours) are maintained by increasing the number of cards issued, maintaining high interest rates, and enlarging the volume of charges, for which the retailers accepting the cards also pay a fee.

To beat them at their own game—to stop paying whatever the traffic will bear—we need to become less dependent on the use of credit cards. Don't accept every credit card you are offered. Never accept a credit card at the normal rate. Why pay an annual fee? Reducing the volume of credit cards in circulation is the only way to get the card issuers to focus on quality and security.

For more information on credit card fraud, call the National Consumer Helpline at the Office of Consumer Affairs at 1-800-664-4435 (10:00 A.M. to 2:00 P.M.).

Embezzlement and the Dishonest Bank Employee

The Falsely Accused

When William Thomas Baskin, a bank manager of Household Bank in Annandale, Virginia, was stealing money from his elderly depositors, he was putting the names and initials of other employees on the paperwork to shift the blame for the transactions.

In that case the deception didn't work. Although investigators were initially very suspicious of the other employees, they were ultimately able to prove that Baskin had made the 23 unauthorized cash withdrawals and was solely responsible for the theft of $26,040.

But not all bank employees who were falsely accused have been so lucky. Some have gone through hell trying to prove their innocence.

Dianne Phelps, perky and pretty, was only 18 years old in 1988 when she got her first real job at the IBM Manassas Employee Federal Credit Union in Manassas, Virginia.

Determined to do a good job and make her mother, a Fairfax police officer, proud, Ms. Phelps worked hard and won the respect of her customers and coworkers.

In fact, she was energetically immersed in her work that day in 1988 when she was called into the president's office.

If Ms. Phelps, bubbling over with youthful enthusiasm, thought the president was going to compliment her on her work or perhaps give her an exciting new assignment, she couldn't have been more wrong.

Federal officers were waiting in the president's office. They ordered her to turn around, placed handcuffs on her wrists, and charged her with embezzling $108,000.

Feeling a wide range of emotions—shock, anger, humiliation, and helplessness—and with tears welling in her eyes, Ms. Phelps was publicly escorted from the bank. She was fingerprinted, photographed, and placed in jail until she could be bailed out a short time later.

In the months that followed her arrest, Ms. Phelps lived under a cloud of suspicion as her reputation was slandered by neighbors, coworkers, and former friends. Her cries of "I didn't do it!" were drowned out by a tidal wave of rumor and ridicule.

Ms. Phelps had neither any warning that she was suspected of anything improper nor any knowledge of the embezzlement until she was called into the president's office.

Day by day for six years Ms. Phelps coped with the gossip and snide remarks, constantly wondered what people were thinking and saying about her, and had a difficult time feeling real joy, despite a new career and a loving fiance. The arrest had changed her life. ·

She was growing angry and cynical. And who could blame her? She was innocent. She had been set up by Linda Ann Godin, her 40-year-old boss.

Ms. Phelps was cleared of the embezzlement in 1995, but her exoneration came about mostly by accident and almost didn't occur at all.

Shortly before 8:00 A.M. on October 19, 1991, Linda Ann Godin, who had been Phelps's boss at the IBM credit union, entered the Independent Bank in Manassas, Virginia, where she was employed as a supervisor, and staged a robbery. She told police that she was knocked unconscious by an unseen intruder, and bank officials reported that $64,000 was missing.

But when medical tests failed to show any sign of assault

and police voiced strong suspicions about Godin's story, bank officials decided to audit her books. Investigators discovered that the $64,000 had been embezzled by Godin, not stolen by an armed robber.

In a plea-bargain agreement, Godin admitted that she had embezzled the $64,000 from the Independent Bank and had also embezzled the $108,000 from the IBM Manassas Employee Federal Credit Union in 1988.

Godin had tampered with Ms. Phelps's teller documents to make it look as though the teenager had stolen the $108,000. By inflating and then rewriting Ms. Phelps's teller summary sheets, Godin had made Ms. Phelps look like an embezzler.

White-collar criminals are notorious for shifting the blame and framing others for their crimes. They are smart and shrewd, corrupt and cunning. They are masters of deception and partners in crime.

Spotting and Stopping Embezzlers

Focusing on armed robberies, the banking industry is ignoring the greater financial threat—the dishonest employee. There are more than 29,000 incidents of embezzlement each year in the United States at banks, savings and loans, and credit unions, thefts that net white-collar criminals $3.5 billion. In contrast, there are about 9000 armed bank robberies each year resulting in about $90 million in losses nationwide.

In a survey of 325 embezzlements, researchers noted that many bank directors acted as if "it could never happen here" and were ignoring even the most obvious danger signs among their employees: drug and alcohol dependency, gambling addictions, hopeless indebtedness, suspicious absenteeism, haphazard adherence to policy and procedures, and employees who flaunted lavish lifestyles beyond their means.

The sampling of 325 embezzlers, 168 of whom were female, also indicated that both male and female supervisors were underestimating the female employee. "Activities that would normally be considered suspicious were ignored or overlooked if the employee was female," explained one investigator.

The banking industry has the knowledge and the power to reduce employee embezzlement by 80 percent. All it needs now is the will to do so.

Tips for Fighting Back

- Individual credit card consumers need to keep a close eye on their accounts. If you see a suspicious charge, call the 800 number on the statement and ask for an explanation. Never give out a credit card number over the phone to an unknown party. Take all receipts and either file or destroy them. Tear up the carbon charge slip, because it contains your card numbers. Don't put your credit card number on the Internet. If your card is missing, immediately call the company that issued it. For more information on credit card fraud call the National Consumer Helpline at the Office of Consumer Affairs at 1-800-664-4435 (10:00 A.M. to 2:00 P.M.).

- Memorize your personal identification number (PIN); do not write the number and leave it where a thief can find it. When using the ATM, don't let those in line behind you see you enter your PIN.

- Banks should provide bank tellers, our first line of defense, with specialized, ongoing fraud awareness training programs.

- Banks have got to make a better effort to guard confidential customer information. If banks could prevent leaks of personal financial information, they would prevent over $500 million in fraud each year.

- Bank customers should be especially concerned about their so-called dormant accounts. When you open an account, especially a money market or savings account, and don't make a deposit or withdrawal for six months, your account becomes dormant. Dormant accounts are the easiest to embezzle from because no one is watching the activity. Always check your statements; don't just throw your unopened envelope into a drawer not to be looked at until tax time. Banks aren't watching your account, so it's up to you.

- Your trust fund is your nest egg. You need to know what the investments are and what income is being earned. Don't assume that the bank has implemented the controls that are necessary to protect your account. Remember, *you* are the primary control. Become complacent and you are particularly vulnerable to being ripped off.

- To guard against dishonest loan officers, banks will have to increase supervision, stop giving approval authority to any one individual, and start implementing standard counterchecks.

- Thousands of bad loans, which have cost taxpayers billions of dollars, indicate that banks and bankers need to get back to basics. Loan information provided by the applicant must be confirmed and verified. Lying to get loans, too many crooks are overstating the value of their assets, exaggerating their income, hiding debts, second mortgages, and other loans, inflating their net worth, and submitting false financial statements under phony names. All loan documents need to be in place before the loan proceeds are disbursed. Did anyone go to the alleged company to check inventory, machinery, and so forth? Did someone talk to the accountant? What about the borrower's character and credit history? Has he or she defaulted on other loans? Wake up, bankers, this isn't Monopoly we are playing! This is no time to relax standards or to approve excessively risky loans.

- Bank fraud cases in all 50 states prove that too many bankers are not checking out important facts before giving away depositors' money. Bankers should stop skipping steps and start investigating the facts before doling out money. The banking system can no longer afford to operate on the honor system or to accept handshakes for collateral.

- Once a loan is properly approved, one of the greatest risks for loss is that money will not be spent or invested as the applicant stated. In Maryland, a bank loaned a 46-year-old man $122,000 to purchase a forklift and a boat. The man spent the money on good times and defaulted on the loan. Naturally, the banks couldn't repossess a forklift and a boat that were never purchased. The borrower simply declared bankruptcy and turned to the rest of us, the U.S. taxpayers, to pay his debt. In another case, a developer defaulted on a $23-million loan which was supposed to be used to build a shopping center.

The developer illegally used half of the loan to create a trust for his children and then concealed the trust with fraudulent financial statements. Most of the losses due to diversions could be headed off if banks confirmed and verified the facts, talked to third parties, and did not advance funds before the collateral was under the control of the bank. Although they boast of advanced business degrees and years of financial experience, many bankers have proven to be incredibly irresponsible.

A P P E N D I X

Chronology

The following white-collar crime cases, listed in reverse chronological order by industry, are excerpted from the author's huge database of incidents. There are thousands upon thousands of more entries that are not printed due to space constraints.

Banking

January 17, 1996—Baltimore, Maryland—The U.S. attorney's office charged developer Dennis A. Laskin, 52, with bank fraud and concealing assets from the Resolution Trust Corporation. The felony charges concern two loans, one for $3.1 million and the other for $20 million, that Laskin took out to finance real estate projects. Laskin defaulted on both loans. Authorities allege that Laskin illegally used more than $10 million of the money to create a family trust and then concealed the trust with fraudulent financial statements when banks and the RTC tried to recover the money.

September 18, 1995—Billerica, Massachusetts—Terry L. Welsh, 34, pleaded guilty to the charges that she embezzled $176,000 from Billerica Municipal Employees Credit Union, where she was the office manager. Mrs. Welsh admitted writing checks to herself and to her husband, and concealing them as payments to vendors or other credit union members.

September 15, 1995—Pittsburgh, Pennsylvania—Sean Hitchman, a 27-year-old bank employee whose job was to refill automated teller machines for the Mellon Bank, is believed to have stolen $1.2 million in cash before skipping the country. Hitchman was captured by Dutch police in Amsterdam on September 22, 1995, as he returned to his room at the Holiday Inn. Police found $45,000 in cash on him and learned that $740,000 was stashed in his car at Pittsburgh International Airport. About $400,000 of the bank's money is still missing.

August 29, 1995—Bowling Green, Kentucky—Richard D. Mangone, 50, head of the defunct Barnstable Credit Union and the Digital Federal Employees Credit Union in Massachusetts, turned himself over to U.S. marshals and FBI agents in Bowling Green after 18 months as a fugitive. Mangone disappeared in February 1994 a week before he was to be sentenced on his July 1993 conviction for money laundering, embezzlement, and bank fraud. He was convicted of bilking the credit unions of $40 million to $75 million through phony mortgage loans, straw sales, and land flips. Mangone, a high-stakes, hotshot gambler, enjoyed spending depositors' money on fancy cars and casinos. On September 12, 1995, Mangone was sentenced to 24 years in prison, the longest federal sentence ever issued for a white-collar crime in Massachusetts.

August 24, 1995—Columbus, Ohio—Rev. John T. Coats II, 27, a member of the staff at the Centenary United Methodist Church and former vice president of the Columbus NAACP chapter, was sentenced to six months in prison and home confinement for stealing $78,825 from National City Bank. Coats and two coconspirators, a man and a woman, used phony names to open accounts in 10 bank branches. The trio then obtained the identification number of a National City Bank employee. Pretending to be the employee, the conspirators telephoned National headquarters, requested the money be transferred into the bogus accounts, and withdrew the cash.

July 26, 1995—Annandale, Virginia—William Thomas Baskin, 48, a manager of Household Bank, was convicted of embezzling $26,040 from the accounts of senior citizens. Baskin put the names and initials of other employees on the paperwork to shift blame for the transactions.

July 24, 1995—Baltimore, Maryland—Michael Clott, a former banker who served seven years in prison for swindling 300 depositors out of $15.7 million, was arrested again while on probation and charged with a scheme that bilked 50 borrowers out of $2 million. After his release from prison in 1994, Clott allegedly began offering unsuspecting borrowers the opportunity to purchase second mortgages through a New Jersey bank. The bank, however, knew nothing about the deals. Authorities believe that Clott used the money he received from his victims to buy a $650,000 home. All the while, he told his probation officer that he was living in a modest apartment and working at a tire company for $300 a week.

July 19, 1995—Upper Darby, Pennsylvania—Jay M. Gross, 74, the former chairman and chief executive officer of the now-defunct Bell Savings Bank, pleaded guilty to funneling $3.4 million in contracts to companies owned and controlled by him. He also pleaded guilty to misapplication of bank funds for loaning $200,000 in Bell money to an associate to buy Bell stock for him because he had already purchased his legal maximum. In 1993 the Resolution Trust Corporation sued Gross and five other Bell executives in an effort to recoup $46.25 million in losses that were the result of unsafe, unsound, and illegal practices.

July 6, 1995—Pasadena, California—Michael Mahoney, a 29-year-old employee of the Bank of Industry, was sentenced to a 21-month prison term after admitting that he accepted $35,477 in bribes for recommending about 20 U.S. Small Business Administration loans. A dozen of the loans went bad, costing taxpayers $2 million. He was also found guilty of embezzling from a second bank.

June 23, 1995—Dade County, Florida—Two years after state regulators closed the Hospital Employees Credit Union, authorities charged Carolyn Choos, 46, the ex-manager, with embezzling $1,642,902. Investigators found that money had been mysteriously shuffled among accounts, that regular statements were not mailed out, and that depositors who insisted on statements were provided with phony ones. The bank first became suspicious of Choos when a part-time coworker reportedly saw her pocket $700 in cash that a depositor brought in. Investigators would learn that Choos, who made $22,000 a year, was extremely generous to friends and acquaintances. She reportedly gave her hairdresser a $14,000 sport utility truck and purchased a $68,000 speedboat for a man who had helped her in a sideline business.

June 21, 1995—Boston, Massachusetts—A federal grand jury indicted Edward S. Buchanan, who once headed the Massachusetts Bank & Trust Co. of Brockton, and charged him with money laundering, misuse of bank funds, conspiracy, and wire fraud. The indictment, replete with references to padded payrolls and ghost employees, alleged that Buchanan used bank funds to purchase a Rolls-Royce Corniche, to pay the salaries and benefits of crew members aboard his yacht, and to buy and insure a Mercedes-Benz and a Jeep Cherokee for two family members. The indictment also cited an alleged investment of $625,000 of bank money in a corporation that owned the yacht. The wire-fraud charge stated that Buchanan transferred $500,000 out of a partnership account without the consent of his two business partners and allegedly used the money to buy stock for himself. In 1989 the Federal Reserve fined Buchanan $1 million for undisclosed violations and in 1992 he was forced to return $170,000 to 40 employees after being charged with misappropriating their pension money.

June 5, 1995—White Plains, New York—John Bald, 31, the manager of the Scarsdale branch of the Dime Savings Bank, pleaded guilty to stealing almost $260,000 from an 86-year-old widow's bank account over six years.

May 26, 1995—Alexandria, Virginia—A federal judge sentenced Linda Ann Godin, 45, to 21 months in prison for embezzling $64,000 from Independent Bank, now Crestar Bank, where she was the evening supervisor. To cover up her theft, Godin had entered the bank and staged a robbery, claiming that she had been knocked unconscious by an unseen intruder. An investigation revealed that Godin also had embezzled $108,000 from the IBM Manassas Federal Credit Union in 1988 and that she had altered the books to throw suspicion on a fellow employee.

May 26, 1995—Philadelphia, Pennsylvania—After five months as a fugitive, Jose Rivera, 48, a former vice president of the Cheltenham Bank, surrendered to police. Rivera was charged with embezzling about $350,000 by transferring money out of two corporate accounts into an account he had opened.

May 15, 1995—Akron, Ohio—Eight people were charged with writing bad checks and manipulating ATMs and electronic banking systems to steal hundreds of thousands of dollars from banks in Columbus, Dayton, Reynoldsburg, Canton, Mansfield, and other cities. Sheriffs were reluctant to release details of the crime because the thefts were accomplished so easily.

Charities

December 13, 1995—Phoenix, Arizona—The *Arizona Republic* reported that a state audit discovered that only 15 of 124 criminal bingo complaints referred to the Department of Public Safety from 1989 to 1994 were investigated. In one case two senior-citizen groups reported that the director of a bingo-funded charity was using bingo funds to make improvements on his home, but the case was never investigated.

December 12, 1995—South Kingstown, Rhode Island—A 44-year-old man was charged with embezzling $8800 from the Nathan Foundation, a group that funds research into sudden infant death syndrome.

December 11, 1995—Washington, D.C.—Seven charities lost a Supreme Court appeal and were ordered to return nearly $500,000 in donations from Michael Douglas, a convicted stock swindler. The Appeals Court likened Douglas' actions to the act of a thief running into a church and dumping the money he just stole into a collection plate. Surely, the thief's victim and not the church would be entitled to that money, the Appeals Court said.

Douglas was sentenced to 12 years in federal prison for stealing $30 million from investors.

October 30, 1995—New York, New York—Police arrested Frank Williams, 54, director of the American Parkinson's Disease Association, and charged him with embezzling more than $870,000 from the charity. The association hired a private investigative firm and notified federal authorities when it began to suspect embezzlement.

October 12, 1995—Washington, D.C.—Lawyer John Diuguid, 63, admitted that he stole $34,622 from the Community Services for Autistic Adults and Children charity and used the money to pay off a personal loan and back rent on his law office.

September 20, 1995—Miami, Florida—Metro-Dade police announced that they were investigating the former director of a charity for the homeless charging that he stole thousands of dollars. The director, who resigned 10 days earlier, was accused of writing checks to former employees, forging their signatures, cashing the checks, and depositing the money into his own bank account. The embezzlement surfaced when a former employee photocopied six checks that she felt were forged. An initial audit uncovered several forged checks and found that 150 canceled checks were missing from the files.

July 27, 1995—Phoenix, Arizona—The FBI arrested four telemarketers who impersonated disabled people to sell garbage bags and first-aid kits at inflated prices. The scam was detected when job applicants for Challenged Workers of America called KNXV-TV and complained that the charity supervisors had coached them to "talk funny" and to "act like you're disabled." Police believe the same suspects got rich pulling off the same scam in Houston, Seattle, and other cities. Quoted in the *Arizona Republic*, Cheryl Becker, executive director of the Mental Health Association of Arizona, said such scams undermine the credibility of legitimate organizations.

July 24, 1995—New York, New York—Four CBS workers were suspended after the *Wall Street Journal* reported that the network was bilked out of thousands of dollars by employees who allegedly set up a phony nonprofit arts foundation charity. The phony charity may have received tens of thousands of dollars over the past several years.

June 22, 1995—Alexandria, Virginia—Former United Way president William Aramony, 67, was sentenced to seven years in federal prison for defrauding the charity of more than $1 million to support a lavish lifestyle. Aramony used the money to purchase luxuries including two condominiums and to travel first class with teenaged girlfriends. Thomas J. Merlo, 64, United Way's chief financial officer, was sentenced to four and a half years in prison, and Stephen J. Paulachak, 49, who headed a nonprofit spinoff that Aramony created, received a two-and-a-half-year sentence.

June 22, 1995—Spring Hill, Florida—Darryl Richard Bruggemann, 33, a Florida-based telemarketer, was arrested and charged with soliciting nearly $200,000 in charitable contributions on behalf of four police and Vietnam War veterans groups that never received a penny. Out-of-state contributors sent money to a mail-forwarding service in their state, which was then passed on to Bruggemann in Florida. Bruggemann was charged with fraud and operating an unlicensed telemarketing business. None of the police or veterans groups were aware of the fund-raising effort.

June 20, 1995—Detroit, Michigan—Susan May, 51, the former comptroller of the defunct Metropolitan Detroit Youth Foundation, pleaded guilty to one count of embezzling at least $5000 from the federally funded charity. She was allowed to plead guilty to only one count even though she admitted to the *Free Press* that she had charged the foundation "about $20,000" for personal expenses. Dennis Gibson, the foundation executive director, told the *Free Press* that May actually embezzled more than $250,000, and he provided a reporter with May's credit card bills showing foundation charges for jewelry, furs, and golf equipment. Richard Ewing, the former associate director of the foundation, cut a deal with federal authorities and was put on probation for embezzling $10,000. A state auditor's probe discovered that the foundation has misspent $1 million. Money earmarked for job training and youth services was allegedly used by charity executives for golf outings, Detroit Pistons tickets, and unauthorized cash bonuses.

May 25, 1995—Nairobi, Kenya—UNICEF's executive director, Carol Bellamy, reported that the United Nations Children's Fund lost as much as $10 million to fraud and mismanagement by its Kenya office in 1993 and 1994. The fraud included payments for nonexistent services, double billing, insurance claims for bogus medical problems, and payments to nonexistent contractors. Blatant mismanagement also cost contributors and the needy millions of dollars. UNICEF managers and employees were clearly guilty of such offenses as overstaffing, overspending for services, and using UNICEF vehicles for personal purposes.

May 15, 1995—Philadelphia, Pennsylvania—The Foundation for New Era Philanthropy, which promised a double-your-money windfall to hundreds of nonprofit institutions and private investors, filed for bankruptcy, listing an incredible $551 million in liabilities and $80 million in assets. The bankruptcy left hundreds of charities in the lurch and threatened many with extinction.

April 18, 1995—Washington, D.C.—Nina K. Solarz, the wife of former Brooklyn Congressman Stephen J. Solarz, pleaded guilty to stealing $7500 from the American Friends of Turkish Women, a charity of which she was president. The embezzlement occurred in 1992 when she wrote a $7500 check to herself without the charity's authorization. Mrs. Solarz, 63, also pleaded guilty to being part of the now-infamous House of Representatives banking scandal. She wrote a $5200 check on her husband's House bank account payable to her son, even though she knew the account was already overdrawn by $10,000. Although the court, in a plea bargain, allowed Mrs. Solarz to plead guilty to only one bad check, she actually bounced hundreds of checks.

February 16, 1995—Walpole, Massachusetts—Harvard graduate Charles K. Lee, 23, was sentenced to one year in prison and ordered to pay full restitution for stealing $119,881.26 from the Jimmy Fund, a charity that funds cancer research for children. As cochairman of "An Evening with Champions," a Jimmy Fund skating exhibition that featured Nancy Kerrigan, Lee was responsible for collecting donations and maintaining the fundraiser's checkbook. But instead of paying the charity, Lee used the contributions to travel, eat at fine restaurants, and purchase fancy clothes and expensive stereo equipment. On February 23, 1995, a second Harvard University student pleaded guilty to stealing from the Jimmy Fund. David G. Sword, 25, admitted that he stole $6838 and was sentenced to a year's probation and 250 hours of community service and ordered to repay the missing funds.

December 21, 1994—Boston, Massachusetts—A federal judge ordered Dr. Bernardo Nadal-Ginard, 52, to repay nearly $6.5 million he misappropriated from the Boston Children's Heart Foundation, a nonprofit organization he had founded in 1982 to conduct research into children's heart disease. Part of the doctor's scam involved a $4 million severance payment he awarded himself even though he had not left his foundation post. A renowned cardiologist, Dr. Nadal-Ginard was the former chairman of the Children's Hospital cardiology department and a former Harvard Medical School professor. In a separate case, he was charged with embezzling more than $400,000 from his practice and from a start-up biotechnology company called Myogenics.

December 14, 1994—Washington, D.C.—Lorna Sammoury, 32, an employee of the United Palestinian Appeal, pleaded guilty to stealing $531,000 by depositing hundreds of checks made out to the charitable organization into her personal banking account. The citizens who contributed the $531,000 believed they were funding medical, educational, and social programs for Palestinians in the West Bank and Gaza.

October 30, 1994—Tampa, Florida—Oscar Guitian, 25, was sentenced to 10 months in jail and ordered to pay restitution to 65 people he cheated out of $100,000. Sixty-five Cuban Americans gave more than $100,000 to Guitian believing that he was sending supplies and cash to their relatives on the Communist island of Cuba. Guitian was actually putting the money in his own pocket.

August 24, 1994—Manhattan, New York—The State Attorney General, G. Oliver Koppell, filed a suit against Carlo Batchelor, who fraudulently raised about $143,000 by claiming to be collecting money for the families of firefighters who had died in the line of duty. Pretending to be a representative of the fire department or the police department, Batchelor contacted small businesses and asked the owners to send contributions by United Parcel Service to an address in Saylorsburg, Pennsylvania. When detectives went to Batchelor's home, his wife, who knew her husband by a different name, explained that he had disappeared but agreed to assist in the investigation.

August 3, 1994—Annapolis, Maryland—Convicted car thief Gino Marchetti Jones, 33, was indicted for selling more than 100 cars, trucks, boats, and campers he allegedly obtained through a phony charity scheme. Authorities said that Jones collected 167 vehicles by soliciting donations to a fraudulent charity called the Baltimore City Therapeutic Fund for Mentally and Physically Challenged Citizens.

March 29, 1994—Montgomery County, Pennsylvania—Nancy Anne Stedman, 41, was sentenced to 11 to 23 months in prison for embezzling $129,627 from the American Lung Association. As director of business affairs and bookkeeper for the local charity, Stedman admitted that she forged checks and doctored expense invoices to make it appear that the money was going to cover mailing expenses. Stedman's attorney tried to absolve her of responsibility by arguing that his client was emotionally immature and suffered from an "adjustment disorder."

February 21, 1994—New York, New York—The *New York Post* reported that four top officials with the American Society for the Prevention of Cruelty to Animals (ASPCA) had been fired because of mismanagement of funds and massive overtime abuses that allowed the employees to triple their base salaries. One investigator whose base salary was $60,000 earned a whopping $192,096 by submitting claims for overtime. The ASPCA receives public and private donations.

Education

January 26, 1996—Bucks County, Pennsylvania—Thomas Donahue, 53, the Bensalem School District facilities manager, was found guilty of forging paperwork and pocketing more than $90,000 in bribes and services on public maintenance contracts he awarded. Convicted of 150 felony counts including bid rigging, Donahue pocketed $15,000 in cash bribes and received more than $75,000 worth of construction done on his Andalusia home. When Donahue received bids for services he frequently tacked on $500 to $1000 for himself, effectively pocketing public funds.

December 1, 1995—Belmont, Massachusetts—A father and son, Jerrold Gibson, 66, and Nathan S. Gibson, 35, were both sentenced to prison terms for directing underlings at University Loan Services, a firm the Gibsons operated, to make false statements on loan histories for federally guaranteed student loans. The Gibsons directed employees to backdate and falsify loan histories and make it appear that they complied with federal requirements. The loans defaulted, costing the U.S. Department of Education $196,879.

August 23, 1995—Los Angeles, California—The University of California filed a lawsuit against Diana Spaniol, 47, a university administrator, charging that she embezzled more than $900,000 while working in the office responsible for protecting the university's assets from fraudulent claims. Spaniol, a manager in UC's Office of Risk Management, allegedly filed and then approved a number of bogus claims that netted her and her daughter a fortune in university funds. The university charges that Spaniol paid herself $175,000 for a claim that was filed on behalf of a fictitious woman named Diana Harvey. Spaniol allegedly fabricated documents describing Harvey as a 33-year-old UC employee who had been assaulted by a professor. In reality, no such professor exists and no such incident ever occurred. The lawsuit alleges that Spaniol gave $439,000 of the embezzled money to her daughter and states that Spaniol sometimes forged letters, purported to be from university lawyers, to give validity to her phony claims. Mrs. Spaniol committed suicide in her home on September 17, 1995.

August 16, 1995—Broward County, Florida—Police arrested Steven Rubin, 28, the trusted transportation director at Hillel Community Day School, and charged him with paying teenagers to write anti-Semitic slogans and to vandalize 16 school buses so he could funnel the repair work on the buses to his father's mechanic shop and a friend's moribund upholstery business. Police arrested Al Rubin, Steven Rubin's father, and accused him of charging the school $16,000 for $200 worth of transmission repairs. Police and a prosecutor said the upholstery shop charged the school $28,000 for repairing the slashed seats in 16 buses, and that by having the teenagers scrawl "Jew," "Hitler," "White Power," and other odious slogans, Rubin apparently wanted his moneymaking scheme to appear to be a hate crime.

June 6, 1995—Concord, Massachusetts—Robert P. O'Keeffe, comptroller of the East Coast Aero Technical School, was sentenced to 27 months in prison for embezzling $1 million. O'Keeffe used the $1 million to buy a new Porsche, speed boat, fishing vessel, and an eye-popping $500,000 model train collection for his basement. Investigators learned that O'Keeffe had been improperly depositing student tuition checks into a petty cash account which he exclusively controlled. From the petty cash account, O'Keeffe wrote checks payable to Shawmut Bank that he deposited into his own accounts. Meanwhile the books looked fine because the tuition checks were recorded as deposited in school accounts.

May 25, 1995—Kent, Washington—According to an Internal Revenue Service audit obtained by the *Seattle Times*, Darlene Jevne, who founded the St. Christopher Academy for children with dyslexia and attention deficit disorders, siphoned off $343,627 of the school's money. Jevne, who was said to have embezzled the funds from 1990 to 1995, reportedly used the money to purchase condominiums in Sun Valley, to renovate a 400-acre Idaho ranch, and to pay for her divorce and other bills.

May 24, 1995—Amherst, Massachusetts—An Essex County grand jury charged a University of Massachusetts insurer with stealing $410,000 from student health accounts. State prosecutors say the alleged theft paid for his rent, golf club expenses, and business costs.

May 10, 1995—Denver, Colorado—East High School Principal Pia E. Smith, 43, pleaded guilty to cashing several school district checks valued at about $9000 and using much of the funds for personal use. In one case she cashed a $4000 check made out to the school district from the Colorado Historical Society and in another case she signed the name of another person without authorization and cashed a check for $2000. Additional checks for smaller amounts were also cashed improperly.

April 17, 1995—Compton, California—Charles Monk, 63, a former school administrator, pleaded guilty to swindling the school district out of $27,461 by approving checks for supplies the district never received. Monk ordered supplies from two fictitious companies and pocketed the money.

April 6, 1995—New York, New York—Antonio Bilbao, the 52-year-old principal of P.S. 142, a grammar school for underprivileged children, pleaded guilty to stealing $11,500 from his students. Bilbao stole cash from the proceeds of a children's bake sale and wrote checks for purchases that were never made on a separate Board of Education fund. He was the third principal in recent months charged with white-collar crimes.

March 31, 1995—Coney Island, New York—Prosecutors charged that Stuart Possner, principal of Public School 100, stole a total of $76,000 and fleeced the school system and his own elementary school students using a variety of illegal schemes. In a lengthy indictment, prosecutors alleged that Possner, who was the 1992 Principal of the Year in his district, pocketed $11,000 his students raised through the sale of candy, that he stole the cash proceeds from a school Valentine's Day dance and a school movie, and that he plundered $4000 worth of school supplies, which he used at a summer camp he operated in the Poconos. The indictment also charged that he got paid for working as a supervisor of an after-school program when he was actually working as a principal for a Jewish religious school and that he forced school employees to make party favors, during working hours, for his son's bar mitzvah and his daughter's sweet 16 party. In separate cases, several teachers charged that Possner coerced them into joining a political club advantageous to him and that he sexually harassed several female teachers.

February 22, 1995—Los Angeles, California—Two former UCLA administrators were indicted for allegedly embezzling more than $600,000 by duping the university into paying two employment agencies, secretly established by the administrators, for work that was never performed. Approximately $220,000 of the stolen funds were said to have been used to build a new wing on one administrator's home.

February 15, 1995—Washington, D.C.—Ann Cooke, 64, an official with the city's public school system, pleaded guilty to embezzling $54,000 from the Neediest Kids charity. Cooke, whose school job was to issue money donated to the charity, bought a leather coat for $1200 and a fox jacket for $1000 and splurged on gems, clothes, and other luxuries from the Home Shopping Network.

February 10, 1995—Los Angeles, California—After first denying the crime, Arnese Clemon, director of the Institute for Successful Living, pleaded guilty to a scheme that defrauded the Los Angeles Unified School District of more than $700,000. Dewey Hughes, a consultant, had pleaded guilty to the same crime on January 30, 1995. Creating phony records, the two pretended to enroll hundreds of phantom students and then collected aid money from the district for each student.

February 1, 1995—Detroit, Michigan—Mack Walker and Ethel Durr, who processed Pell Grant loans totaling $2 million for the Walker Education Center, pleaded guilty to falsifying applications and other fraud charges.

January 20, 1995—Wayne County, Michigan—Mary Ann Brueggemann, a 59-year-old treasurer for the Holy Cross Lutheran Elementary School, pleaded no contest to embezzling $363,000. The embezzlement forced the 67-year-old school to close. Investigators learned that Brueggemann had written 185 illegal checks to herself and to "cash." Like most white-collar criminals, Brueggemann was quick to blame others. "If the board of trustees had done an audit I would probably not have been tempted," she said.

Insurance

December 13, 1995—Baltimore, Maryland—Hamilton A. Schmidt, 41, chief executive officer of the Charter Group Inc., one of Maryland's largest independent insurance agencies, pleaded guilty to stealing $917,393 from his firm. When auditors discovered that the money was missing on September 14, 1993, Schmidt vanished, leaving about 100 workers without their retirement savings. By the time Schmidt was caught 18 months later, Charter's assets were sold, the company had fallen into bankruptcy, and the employee stock ownership plan had collapsed. In his first year as president Schmidt had given himself unauthorized bonuses totalling $409,000 and withdrawn more than $200,000 from the company by booking the funds as short-term loans.

November 3, 1995—Fargo, North Dakota—Police arrested an Iranian immigrant and charged her with arson for insurance, endangering, and making a false report. On October 23, 1995, she asserted that she had been the victim of a vicious hate crime when police found her bound, slashed, and apparently left to die in a fire at her family's Middle Eastern restaurant. Police said that they believed that the woman staged the entire incident to collect insurance money.

October 16, 1995—Montgomery County, Maryland—James Edward Perry, 47, was sentenced to death for the hired-gun murders of nurse Janice Saunders, 38, Mildred Horn, 43, and her eight-year-old quadriplegic son Trevor Horn. Prosecutors said that the murder-for-hire plot was engineered by the boy's father, Lawrence T. Horn, 55, because he stood to inherit nearly $2 million that had been awarded his son in a lawsuit settlement with Children's Hospital.

October 15, 1995—El Reno, Oklahoma—James W. Lewis, 49, the leading suspect in the 1982 poisoned Tylenol episode that killed seven people, was released from prison after serving 12 years for trying to extort money from Johnson & Johnson. Although it was never proven that Lewis, an unemployed accountant, had placed the cyanide in the Tylenol capsules, he did admit to sending a letter to Johnson & Johnson demanding $1 million "to stop the killing." The seven Tylenol deaths toughened criminal penalties for illegal tampering with consumer products and tightened federal regulations for packaging nonprescription drugs.

September 21, 1995—Chicago, Illinois—George Lindemann Jr., 31, acclaimed equestrian and son of one of the richest men in America, was convicted of ordering the killing of his show horse, Charisma, in 1990 to collect $250,000 in insurance money. A codefendant, Marion Hulick, 60, the trainer and manager at the Lindemann family's horse farm in Connecticut, was convicted of the same charges. George Lindemann Jr., whose family fortune is estimated at $600 million, is the son of cellular telephone magnate George Lindemann. The younger Lindemann paid Mrs. Hulick and a man named Tom Burns, aka Tim Ray, a total of $25,000 to kill Charisma. After attaching electric cables, Burns electrocuted the horse.

September 19, 1995—Loudoun County, Virginia—Cassondra Betancourt, 33, was found guilty of murdering her 65-year-old boyfriend, Walter Montague, after she took out a $500,000 life insurance policy on him. Although police originally thought Montague had died of a heart attack, they later learned that Betancourt had poisoned him by putting a massive amount of cocaine in his drink. Betancourt had spent several months trying to convince Montague to get life insurance. When underwriters told her that a girlfriend could not be listed as a dependent, she set up a phony company and applied for business-related life insurance on Montague. In 1987, Betancourt had received a $149,000 life insurance payout after her two-month-old daughter allegedly died of sudden infant death syndrome.

August 28, 1995—Richmond, Virginia—Police arrested Lloyd Mitchell Weaver Jr., a 24-year-old insurance claim clerk, and charged him with using bogus claims to steal $560,000 from his employer, Trigon Blue Cross Blue Shield. He was arrested while trying to withdraw $180,000 at a Crestar Bank branch. Weaver allegedly manipulated an unwitting policyholder's account to cash dozens of checks ranging from $2200 to $93,000 apiece. Investigators learned that Weaver spent $56,000 on a new Range Rover and purchased a 1995 turbo Volvo 850 for $30,000. Weaver allegedly stored $247,000 of the embezzled money in checking, money market, and mutual fund accounts. About $230,000 remained unaccounted for.

August 20, 1995—Monroeville, Alabama—Stanley Kidd, who was convicted of murdering his twin 14-month-old daughters so that he could avoid paying $806 a month in child support and could collect on a $16,000 life insurance policy, was sentenced to two consecutive life terms. Prosecutors said Kidd placed the toddlers in their car seats and pumped carbon monoxide fumes into his car. Kidd was reportedly furious that authorities had started withholding money from his paycheck to pay for child support.

August 14, 1995—Denver, Colorado—Insurance agent John Bryan Jr., 52, who called himself an estate planner and stole $106,000 from a 101-year-old man and his wife, was spared prison so that he could earn money to pay his needy victims, Norman and Susan Pasnow, $700 a month in restitution. Bryan, who received power of attorney from the couple, looted Mr. Pasnow's checking account and his stocks. Pasnow did not recall ever signing a power of attorney agreement. Bryan opened a special mailbox and had all the Pasnows' mail forwarded to him so that he maintained absolute control.

July 26, 1995—Miami, Florida—Ten employees at the department of Health and Rehabilitative Services were charged with forging doctors' signatures and using phony medical bills to defraud an insurance company. The ten workers, including three supervisors, faked injuries and got refund checks ranging from $700 to $7200.

June 30, 1995—Silver Spring, Maryland—David L. Tully, 43, admitted to helping a roommate with AIDS get a life insurance policy by taking a physical in the roommate's name. Tully was caught when he attempted to claim $730,000 from the Mutual Life Insurance Co. after his roommate died.

June 13, 1995—Patterson, New York—A woman who reported her Cadillac stolen and then received $16,000 in insurance money was arrested after the car was found buried 13 feet deep in her backyard. Patricia Tanzi, 45, was charged with grand larceny and insurance fraud. Investigators say the hole was dug with heavy equipment.

June 9, 1995—Northampton, Massachusetts—Suzanne D'Amour, 34, was arrested and charged with hiring a hit man to kill her husband, 55-year-old dentist Robert D'Amour, allegedly so that she could collect on a $3-million life insurance policy. Police said they found a photo of alleged hit man Alex Rankins in the widow's dresser drawer. Prosecutors contended that Rankins, a 48-year-old bartender, was romantically involved with Mrs. D'Amour. The murder victim was the son of Paul D'Amour, cofounder of Big Y Foods, and reportedly inherited a fortune.

June 9, 1995—Portland, Oregon—Two men and a woman who said they were targets of a hate crime were charged with painting swastikas on their own apartment building and later setting the building on fire to collect $50,000 in insurance money.

June 6, 1995—Los Angeles, California—A jury found David Hooker, 33, a former convict, guilty of first-degree murder in the 1993 arson death of his father, a retired police sergeant. Thomas

Warren Hooker, who was once awarded the LAPD Medal of Valor for rescuing a family from a burning building, died after his son set fire to his home in a scheme to collect insurance money.

June 5, 1995—Santa Barbara, California—Devin Charles Park, 36, was ordered to pay $4 million and spend 63 months in jail for stealing funds from two title insurance companies he managed, Trico Title Co. and Homestead Title Corp. Using his position as president, Park forged signatures, stole customers' escrow funds (money held as collateral in special bank accounts), and used the money to purchase country club memberships, stocks, bonds, stereo equipment, and other personal items.

June 4, 1995—Los Angeles, California—State and local police arrested 46 suspects involved in an auto insurance fraud ring that arranged for uninsured drivers who had car accidents to obtain backdated insurance policies. For $1000, the ringleader of a Hollywood insurance company was providing uninsured motorists with auto insurance policies backdated to a few days before the date of their car accidents so that the drivers could file claims for damages and injuries. The illegal claims, which ranged from $1000 to over $35,000, cost insurance companies $410,000.

May 30, 1995—New City, New York—Michelle Lennon, 24, was sentenced to 20 years to life in prison for murdering her husband, Brooke Lennon, a 54-year-old senior vice president for the Grand Union supermarket chain in Wayne, N.J. Prosecutors believe that she committed the murder in order to collect on a $2-million life insurance policy and the $280,000 that her husband had in the bank. Michelle Lennon, who never showed any remorse, admitted that she beat her husband with a baseball bat, placed a plastic bag over his head, and then strangled him with a telephone cord. She and her 26-year-old boyfriend then disposed of the body.

Lawyers

February 1, 1996—Alexandria, Virginia—The U.S. Attorney's Office began investigating a well-known real estate attorney who allegedly stole $3.5 million from at least 25 clients. Attorneys involved in the investigation believe that the attorney may have kept the proceeds from house sales instead of sending the money to the sellers' lenders to pay off old mortgages. To keep the scheme from being detected, the lawyer reportedly continued to make monthly payments on the sellers' mortgages, without the sellers' knowledge. In some cases, he allegedly told mortgage companies to send all future bills to his address. The scheme unraveled when several sellers discovered that their loans had not been paid off.

January 25, 1996—Greenfield, Massachusetts—Lewis Metaxas was ordered to serve six months in jail for bilking two clients out of nearly $30,000. Prosecutors said Metaxas took money from a man convicted of drunken driving by claiming he could get the man a special license. Another client gave Metaxas $15,000 to settle a paternity suit, but the lawyer pocketed the money.

December 4, 1995—Miami, Florida—Miami defense lawyer Harvey Robbins, 69, was sentenced to four years in prison and fined $50,000 for tax fraud and for helping drug smugglers hide their money from the IRS. Among other tricks, Robbins used his wife's name on documents for shell companies he established to shield his clients' drug money from the IRS. Robbins, who filed false tax returns for himself, also accepted $475,000 from a major drug dealer to purchase bearer bonds, securities that do not show the names of their true owners. Robbins is just one of hundreds of lawyers who are suspected of laundering money for drug traffickers in recent years.

November 24, 1995—Central Falls, Rhode Island—A state representative and lawyer was charged with stealing about $70,000 from an estate he administered. The attorney, who was suspended from practicing law, said that he only borrowed the money.

October 17, 1995—Manhattan, New York—A disbarred lawyer was charged with stealing more than $1 million by embezzling from estates, keeping insurance money awarded to clients, pocketing down payments for real estate transactions, and forging names on estate documents. He was charged with stealing $127,000 from the estate of a deceased priest and pocketing $57,000 in damages that were awarded to a 90-year-old woman after a car accident.

October 11, 1995—Dade County, Florida—Personal injury lawyer Arthur Garel, 47, pleaded guilty to embezzling $186,500 from his own law firm and stealing at least $87,000 in client settlement checks. His victims included his aunt and son, a mentally handicapped man, and a policeman who had sued his marriage counselor for having an affair with his wife. Guilty of fraud, three counts of theft, and 20 counts of check forgery, Garel was sentenced to 364 days in prison. Garel did not pay one penny out-of-pocket to reimburse the firm or his clients and will not have a conviction on his record.

September 29, 1995—Sacramento, California—A prosperous attorney with offices in California and Florida was charged in federal court with mail and tax fraud in connection with a scheme that cheated legal clients and health insurance companies out of $18 million. A representative of the attorney says his client intended to plead guilty and to resign from the bar.

September 28, 1995—Alexandria, Virginia—Two prominent real estate attorneys, Jay N. Eskovitz, 48, and John F. Pitrelli, 47, both pleaded guilty to setting up secret second mortgages ("silent seconds") for home buyers who otherwise wouldn't have been able to obtain first-trust loans and to making false statements to financial institutions. First-trust lenders need to know about other loans because "silent seconds" increase the likelihood of default.

Seven of the "silent second" deals went into foreclosure, resulting in total losses to lenders of $120,000 to $200,000.

September 28, 1995—Newark, New Jersey—Federal officials charged a county prosecutor with 33 counts that included tax evasion, blackmail, extortion, and forging documents so that his son could obtain financial aid for college. Accused of being as crooked as the people he had sent to prison, he was also charged with embezzling $246,000 from two gas stations he owned with other partners. Prosecutors alleged that he repeatedly broke the law "to live a lifestyle far beyond his legitimate means."

September 21, 1995—Manhattan, New York—A grand jury indicted 47 people, including 21 lawyers and two law firm employees, in a scheme to defraud insurance companies by bribing claims adjusters to inflate settlements. Those who were indicted are suspected of being involved in $39 million worth of settlements.

September 21, 1995—Manhattan, New York—Lawyer Harvey Weinig, 47, pleaded guilty to taking part in a $19-million money-laundering operation for the Cali cocaine cartel in Colombia. Weinig told the judge that he was brought into the scheme by his former law partner, Robert Hirsch, who also pleaded guilty. Weinig, Hirsch, and a third man collected drug money from couriers and deposited the money in bank accounts in New York and Switzerland.

September 21, 1995—Tucson, Arizona—The State Bar of Arizona disbarred Richard B. Arrotta, 46, after he admitted that he paid a state claims adjuster $422,000 in bribes for confidential information, including the names of people who had potential liability claims against the state. In a plea bargain Arrotta agreed to pay about $800,000 in fines, and he faces as much as five years in prison. The bribes reportedly earned Arrotta $1.1 million in legal fees.

September 13, 1995—White Plains, New York—Kenneth Gribetz, 51, the flamboyant district attorney of Rockland County, was fined $10,000 and sentenced to five years' probation and 500 hours of community service for tax evasion and for using investigators for personal errands. Gribetz, who cowrote a book about his career, *Murder Along the Way*, admitted failing to report on his tax returns $36,000 that he received in referral fees. He was ordered to repay a total of $44,618.

September 11, 1995—Brooklyn, New York—Lawyer Jeffrey Chodorow, co-owner of the now-defunct Braniff International Airlines, pleaded guilty to charges of conspiracy and defrauding the government in connection with the bankruptcy and collapse of the carrier, which left thousands of employees, ticket holders, and creditors in the lurch. The indictment charged that Chodorow participated in a lucrative kickback and money-laundering scheme and that he defrauded the U.S. Department of Transportation, obstructed justice, and concealed assets from creditors.

August 22, 1995—Flint, Michigan—Attorney Donald D. Rogers was disbarred and ordered to repay $139,960 he stole from the estate of Paul Hathaway, who died in 1992. Hathaway's wife, Minnie, was the sole heir; but instead of placing her inheritance into a trust account for her, Rogers put the money in his personal account.

August 4, 1995—Tampa, Florida—Norbert Schlei, 66, an Assistant Attorney General under Presidents John F. Kennedy and Lyndon B. Johnson, was sentenced to five years in prison for securities fraud in a case involving billions of dollars in fake Japanese government bonds. Prosecutors said that Schlei and five others schemed to sell $16 billion worth of counterfeit Japanese bonds.

July 28, 1995—Jenkintown, Pennsylvania—Disbarred personal injury lawyer David M. Weinfeld, 40, admitted that he stole millions of dollars from his working-class clients. Weinfeld, who represented mostly laborers, negotiated huge group settlements ($2.5 million, $706,000, and $142,000) for hundreds of clients who became ill working with asbestos. Instead of giving the money to his clients, Weinfeld spent the money on personal luxuries and then declared bankruptcy to help protect himself financially.

July 28, 1995—Washington, D.C.—The District of Columbia bar disciplinary authorities recommended the disbarment of Michael X. Morrell, 51, after they found that he had defrauded a French pharmaceutical company by using "tens of thousands—if not hundreds of thousands—of dollars" of its funds to pay for personal expenses including MasterCard and Visa bills, Georgetown basketball tickets, and athletic club memberships. Morrell, who served on the prestigious Board of Regents at Georgetown Law School, was also fired from the law firm Akin, Gump, Strauss, Hauer & Feld. The law firm, which accused Morrell of numerous misdeeds, had to pay a $3.2-million settlement to Morrell's client, Laboratoires Besins Iscovesco.

July 24, 1995—Rockville, Maryland—Michael A. Leiberman, 51, an attorney and certified public accountant, was convicted of laundering more than $700,000 for the leader of a major marijuana distribution ring.

July 20, 1995—Long Island, New York—A wealthy lawyer and financial adviser for the Colombo crime family was indicted and charged with racketeering, extortion, embezzlement, fraud, money laundering, and tax evasion. Investigators say that he, in addition to other crimes, laundered at least $5 million for the Colombo family and cheated four banks, two insurance companies, and two physicians of more than $1 million.

June 28, 1995—Chester County, Pennsylvania—John Emerson High, 47, a lawyer and former Valley Township supervisor, pleaded guilty to stealing $95,295 from seven clients. The lawyer commingled money entrusted to him by seven clients into a banking account in his name and then wrote $95,295 worth of checks payable to cash. High spent all but $85 of his clients' money.

June 28, 1995—Little Rock, Arkansas—Lawyer Webster L. Hubbell, 47, a confidant and consultant to President Bill Clinton and former law partner of Hillary Rodham Clinton, was sentenced to 21 months in prison for mail fraud and tax evasion and for stealing at least $394,000 from clients, taxpayers, and his own partners at the Rose Law Firm.

Medicine

September 19, 1995—Long Island, New York—The owner of an ambulette company was charged with bilking Medicaid out of $442,000 by billing for 9000 fake ambulance rides. State Attorney General Dennis Vacco charged that in at least 43 cases the private ambulance company submitted bills for patients who had died. One reason the alleged fraud was able to continue for five years was because the system had no way to spot bogus invoices.

August 24, 1995—Boston, Massachusetts—Three former executives of C. R. Bard Inc., one of the world's largest health-care products companies, were convicted of conspiring to conceal deadly flaws in artery catheters that have been responsible for two deaths, and using heart patients as human guinea pigs. The convictions came two years after Bard pleaded guilty to 391 fraud charges and paid the government $61 million in fines, a sum equal to the company's gross revenues from the faulty catheters.

August 22, 1995—Howard County, Maryland—Psychiatrist Adul Rermgosakul, 51, was ordered to pay $235,000 in restitution and fines for fraudulently billing Medicaid for therapy sessions that never took place. He was also sentenced to five years in prison, with all but 30 days suspended. Undercover investigators discovered that Dr. Rermgosakul was seeing patients for no longer than three minutes but was billing Medicaid for a 50-minute session. In 1987, Dr. Rermgosakul was ordered to repay $40,000 after being sanctioned for exaggerating on Medicaid bills.

August 18, 1995—Chicago, Illinois—Denny Pitts, 37, who impersonated a doctor to obtain nearly $50,000 worth of AIDS treatment drugs that he then sold on the street, was sentenced to eight years in prison. Pretending to be "Dr. Ramos," Pitts charged controlled substances such as Tylenol No. 4 with codeine to the Department of Public Aid by using stolen public aid patient numbers.

August 1, 1995—Newton, Massachusetts—Rejecting an insanity defense, a jury convicted psychiatrist Richard Skodnek of fraudulently billing Medicare and private insurers $500,000 for patients he never treated. Skodnek routinely made up diagnoses for patients he had never seen and billed insurers for nonexistent sessions. Many victims who were unknowingly labeled as having severe psychological problems worry that the false information, recorded in insurance databases, will come back to haunt them.

July 31, 1995—Miami, Florida—FBI agents arrested 18 South Florida residents and charged them with filing more than $20 million in bogus Medicare claims by billing for medical treatments, equipment, and nutritional supplements that patients never received. The group was also charged with buying patient billing numbers and paying doctors to sign billing requests for patients they never examined. Jose M. Ferrer, 22, was charged with setting up a phony company, of which he was the CEO and sole employee, and stealing $2 million from Medicare. He was accused of paying doctors to sign phony Medicare claims that provided $365 for oxygen treatments and $3150 for medical equipment the elderly patients didn't need or receive. Eleven of the defendants allegedly created 18 separate companies solely to bill Medicare for milk supplements.

July 19, 1995—Washington, D.C.—The General Accounting Office drafted a report stating that First American Health Care, the largest U.S. provider of home medical care for the elderly, submitted $14 million in improper billings. The billings included beer for supervisors and country club fees. After a 19-month investigation, the GAO accused First American of forging medical records, billing the government for gifts given to physicians in exchange for patient referrals, and continuing to visit homes even when patients objected.

May 24, 1995—Miami, Florida—Following a three-year investigation by the FBI and the Florida Department of Insurance, the owner of three medical clinics was arrested on charges that he cheated Medicare, Medicaid, and private insurance companies out of $6.5 million. The clinics allegedly paid bounties to recruiters who rounded up patients willing to fake injuries and ailments for bogus insurance claims. The man and his staff are also accused of running a sideline scam—staging car crashes to cheat insurance companies.

May 16, 1995—Aberdeen, Maryland—Dr. Anibal Britos-Bray, 64, pleaded guilty to billing Medicaid for more than $40,000 for electrocardiograms, throat cultures, X rays, and other medical tests he never performed. Dr. Britos-Bray received a five-year suspended sentence and was ordered to pay $125,000 in restitution. In one case, he billed Medicaid for hip X rays for a patient who complained of a sore finger.

May 4, 1995—Miami, Florida—Cardiologist Jaime A. Vergel, 62, surrendered to federal marshals after being indicted on charges that he and medical technicians Maria Lourdes Prohias and Roberto Sacasas bilked Medicare out of $4 million. The three are accused of billing Medicare for unnecessary or unperformed treatments. Dr. Vergel was released on $500,000 bond.

May 3, 1995—Boston, Massachusetts—Geoffrey S. Bradley, 38, an executive with Providers Inc., pleaded guilty to billing Medicare for at least $4.4 million in phony claims. Since the amount reimbursed by Medicare for medical supplies varies from state to state, Bradley set up shell offices in the six states where payments were the highest.

The bills were sent to those states whether or not the supplies were sold there. The $4.4-million loss was for Massachusetts alone. Bradley is cooperating with authorities, who expect to charge others.

April 27, 1995—Miami, Florida—Dr. Ricardo Samitier, a cosmetic surgeon who was already serving a five-year sentence for letting a patient bleed to death, was sentenced to 26 months in federal prison for defrauding Medicare out of $441,000. Dr. Samitier billed Medicare for scores of patients he never saw and signed Medicare forms for several medical companies that charged Medicare for unnecessary diagnostic tests and for equipment the patients didn't need. Havana-born Samitier said he contributed the stolen money to anti-Castro Cuban exile groups.

April 18, 1995—Boston, Massachusetts—Chiropractor Alan S. Rosenthal, 38, and his wife, Caterina A. Rosenthal, pleaded guilty to illegally assisting scores of people to receive tens of thousands of dollars in insurance payments for phony injuries allegedly suffered in automobile and work accidents. Alan Rosenthal, whose brother was convicted on similar fraud charges in the 1980s, was sentenced to 15 months in jail and agreed to forfeit his chiropractor's license for 30 months. Caterina Rosenthal was given two years' probation.

April 13, 1995—Brookline, Massachusetts—A graduate of Columbia University's medical school was arrested and charged with illegally dispensing prescriptions to drug abusers and others and charging Medicare $100,000 a year. Following the arrest, the state Board of Registration in Medicine voted to suspend the doctor's license. The board discovered that he had repeatedly prescribed tranquilizers to patients with substance abuse problems and that two of his patients had died. Undercover officers posing as patients reported that the doctor engaged in small talk for about 10 minutes and then, without taking a medical history or performing a psychiatric examination, gave them prescriptions for tranquilizers.

April 10, 1995—Wilkes-Barre, Pennsylvania—Pharmacist George G. Kaufer, 49, pleaded guilty to charging the state's Medicaid program for brand name drugs while actually providing less expensive generic drugs to recipients. He submitted bills that falsely indicated that brand name drugs had been specifically requested by the prescribing physicians. Kaufer was placed on 23 months of probation and ordered to pay a $6500 fine.

April 3, 1995—Phoenix, Arizona—Sherron Annette Hanna, 52, a bookkeeper for Dr. Paul Petelin, pleaded guilty to a charge of computer fraud, admitting that she devised a scheme to make false computer entries over a five-year period and stole $436,000.

March 31, 1995—New Orleans, Louisiana—Michael O'Keefe, 63, a former state senate president who was incarcerated in the 1980s for fraud, was charged with scamming physicians out of more than $7.5 million in malpractice premiums. O'Keefe and others were accused of diverting money belonging to doctors to themselves and companies they controlled.

Religion

December 7, 1995—Anne Arundel County, Maryland—A federal grand jury indicted David Robinson on charges of defrauding Rev. Morris Vickers and other ministers out of $700,000. Robinson allegedly persuaded Vickers and others to pool their resources for a number of investments that turned out to be scams. The ministers didn't know that Robinson, articulate and well dressed, had misrepresented himself as a licensed attorney and been convicted in 1989 of defrauding businesses of more than $70,000.

November 17, 1995—Pasadena, California—William R. Jones, the newly appointed treasurer of the California Pacific Conference of the United Methodist Church, was relieved of his duties after it was discovered that he had embezzled at least $350,000 while working in New York for the General Board of Global Ministries of the United Methodist Church. Although Jones wrote four very questionable checks, the bulk of the stolen money was transferred electronically in a single transaction.

August 10, 1995—Montgomery County, Maryland—Lester I. Kaplan, 48, the former executive director of the Jewish Community Center of Greater Washington, pleaded guilty to helping embezzle nearly $1 million. He was one of four officials who were forced to resign after the Jewish Community Center accused them of stealing funds. Jay Arthur Manchester, 51, former chief financial officer, pleaded guilty in May 1995 to four counts of theft. A bookkeeper and a building superintendent worked out a plea-bargain agreement with prosecutors. The four men paid inflated rates to a cleaning company and then siphoned off huge amounts of money. Kaplan also admitted helping Craig M. Shniderman, a professional fund-raiser and former director of Jewish Social Services, steal property from the center's gift shop. After being forced to resign, Shniderman took a job with a charity group that provides food and services to AIDS patients.

May 1, 1995—New York, New York—The Episcopal Church's national office announced that Ellen Cooke, the trusted treasurer and wife of Rev. Nicholas T. Cooke, rector of St. John's Episcopal Church in McLean, Virginia, had embezzled at least $2.2 million from the church and its parishioners over a five-year period. On January 24, 1996, Cooke, 52, admitted in court that she had embezzled the money but claimed she was mentally ill and could not remember much of what she did.

March 28, 1995—Mountain Lakes, New Jersey—Shortly after investigators questioned him about the January 9, 1995, murders of Susan and Lowell Engel, it appears that Rev. James S. Castria aimed his car at a highway abutment and committed suicide. Police believe that Rev. Castria looted the couple's life savings, lured them from their senior citizens' apartment on Staten Island, drove them to the Pennsylvania Poconos, and bludgeoned them to death. Rev. Castria, who had performed the elderly couple's marriage ceremony in 1988, apparently siphoned off their money after inducing them to share a bank account with him.

March 15, 1995—Hagerstown, Maryland—After being caught stealing $183,364 from the Salem Reformed Church, Michael Allen Creek, 42, the former treasurer of the church, was placed on probation and ordered to pay the money back. He had written 10 checks to himself, depleting the church funds, and used the money to build up a private business. The judge ordered Creek to pay the church $30,000 per year for five years.

March 3, 1995—Sebring, Florida—Police arrested Rev. John Canning, 58, the pastor of the multidenominational Fountain of Life Church, and charged him with the murders of Leo and Hazel Gleese. The 90-year-old couple were killed after they discovered that Rev. Canning had abused the power of attorney they gave him and had allegedly stolen tens of thousands of dollars from their bank accounts.

February 25, 1995—Lansing, Michigan—An insurance agent was arraigned on charges of embezzling $479,000 from an account that supports retired Catholic priests. Authorities stated that they believed that he actually embezzled about $979,000 of the diocesan checks from 1984 to 1994, but because of the statute of limitations, he could only be charged with taking five checks worth $479,000 since October 1989.

February 10, 1995—Farmington, Utah—Rev. Raymond Sarter, 50, a Foursquare Pentecostal minister who once headed the Open Door Ministry, was sentenced to 180 days in jail for falsifying 66 money orders worth $3875.

December 16, 1994—Miami, Florida—Antonio Arguedas, 38, was sentenced to nine years in prison for conspiring to defraud two churches of the Assemblies of God out of $125,000. Arguedas and his wife Martha convinced the pastors that they could obtain multimillion-dollar grants from the U.S. State Department's "Pro-Religion Development Fund" if the churches would put up a $125,000 advance payment. To bolster their credibility, Martha pretended to be a successful cardiologist and Antonio pretended to be an international financier. Both churches lost nearly all the money in their coffers. The government seized the couple's assets, which were worth less than $10,000. There is little hope the congregations will be reimbursed.

December 1, 1994—Hendersonville, North Carolina—Television evangelist Jim Bakker, who bilked 118,000 of his loyal PTL followers out of $158 million, was released from prison after serving only 4½ years of his original 45-year sentence. Adding to the collapse of the Praise The Lord ministry was the disclosure that Bakker had engaged in a scandalous affair with sexy church secretary Jessica Hahn and then diverted $265,000 of his followers' money in an unsuccessful attempt to buy her silence.

November 28, 1994—Rochester, New York—The Rev. Patrick Moloney, 62, a Catholic priest, was convicted of conspiring to hide some of the $7.4 million stolen by masked gunmen from a Brink's armored-car depot on January 5, 1993. FBI agents and police raided Father Moloney's mission and apartment on November 12, 1993, and seized about $2.2 million. Nearly $5.2 million is still unaccounted for.

Index